INTRODUCTION

Some of the things I wrote in my first three books seem cringe-worthy looking back, but I don't allow myself much shame. I wrote every word. I stand by every word, because to apologize for something I wrote would be to apologize for a moment in time.

How can I apologize for my thoughts and feelings, now or in the past? How can I say I was thinking the wrong thing? Or that I said the wrong thing? There is no wrong thing. There is only the thing that you said in the moment that you said it.

Some of what I've said in the past has been controversial. I'm sure much of what I say in the future will be similarly controversial. However, nothing you will read here was designed to merely create controversy. I hope that you bear that in mind as you read through this compilation of my three published books—'Scumbag: Musings of a Subhuman,' 'In Defense of Evil: Why Good is Bad and Bad is Good,' and 'Neckbeard Uprising.'

Each one has faults and failings. Each one is an imperfect work. Scumbag is short and more written to be funny or crude than to be enlightening (the version here is not complete. I don't have a complete version, sadly). In Defense of Evil is distracted from its premise early on and never really coheres. Neckbeard Uprising is admittedly cobbled together from conversations I've had on the internet. None of these books represent me or my true potential. But they are the books I've written and I cannot run from them. They may not be everything I wish they were, but they are still my books. And I love them, flaws and all.

I hope you will too.

SCUMBAG:
musings of a subhuman

SCUMBAG:
musings of a subhuman

Written and Illustrated By
The Amazing Atheist

This work is dedicated to Hardcase, for being exactly like me and yet my complete opposite (and for amusing me with his frequent death threats).

**It is also dedicated to Britt Marble—
the only person who has ever met me.**

***

Apart from those two brilliant souls, I'd like to thank a number of those who have shaped me into what I am (for better or for worse):

- Mom, for trying to understand.
- Dad, for supporting my lazy ass.
- Scotty, for being my best friend.
- Stevie, for loving me more than I deserve.
- Cookie, for making me laugh.
- Sheri, for allowing my penis inside her on a few occasions.
- Steve, for trying his best.
- JD, for being wise in his insanity.
- Nick, for making my childhood interesting.
- Natalie, for thinking of others before herself.
- Zac, for his inspiring paintings.
- Cody, for his beautiful photography.
- Nate, for his tireless cruelty.
- Mr. Taylor, for being the biggest asshole I ever met.
- Jesse, for being the first person I ever trusted.

Thank you all.

This is where you'd normally find copyright information, but I'm too fucking lazy to bother with all that jazz—and with the advent of the internet, it would be too much of a pain in the ass to try to stop you from swiping this shit and reusing it anyway. I'll just ask really politely that you not do so and hope that that's enough.

COVER IMAGE: Cody Weber & The Amazing Atheist

A BRIEF LETTER TO MY FANS

> "You know, I thought you were a decent guy until [you insulted me]; now I know you're no different than the dickheads you rant about. Hell, if you're like this to someone whose nice to you, I don't want to know what you're like to your haters."
> -*rdawkinsbulldog, youtube user*

It's fairly safe to say that I'm an asshole.

I make no secret of my petty and spiteful nature, nor do I feel any inclination to improve my personality in the near future. In this age, whether you're a famous movie star with millions of fans, or just some guy who rants on youtube for an audience of a few thousand, people build illusions of you in their minds, convince themselves that they know and understand you; worse, they come around to the belief that, because they are supportive of the work you produce, you are in some way obligated to them.

I owe you nothing. You don't watch my videos out of some sense of charity—you watch them to be amused, enlightened or perhaps even just to mock me. Even now, I owe you nothing. "But I bought your book!" you protest in your nasally whine, tears oozing from the dull cattle-like orbs of your eyes. Yes, you gave me money and, in return, I gave you a book. Transaction over.

Feel free to send me anything you like: your "constructive criticisms", lengthy letters about your personal problems, your poetry, your artwork—whatever. Send me these things until you cum from the sheer joy of it, but **<u>do not</u>** expect me to care or to respond. Sometimes I will, and other times I won't. It depends on my mood.

Now, if you happen to be an attractive female who wishes to pose naked for me, I want you to know that my inbox is always wide open to receive any number of pictures you may choose to fill it with. This is not at all contingent upon my mood—I've never in my life not been in the mood to see a nice set of tits or a cute ass.

And guys, it's okay to take pictures of your girlfriend while she sleeps and send them to me as well. I don't mind at all. No matter how busy my schedule becomes, you have my solemn vow that I will make time to view photos of your sleeping, unsuspecting girlfriend who has no idea what a scumbag her boyfriend happens to be.

In fact, it doesn't even have to be your girlfriend. If you've got a sister or a mom or a neighbor that you want to send me pictures of, that's all good too.

For that matter, the pictures don't even have to be of girls. A lot of guys these days are pretty effeminate. If I take my glasses off, I can't even tell the difference.

I'm really not picky. I mean, if you could just send me close up pictures of your knees pressed together to kind of look like an ass, I can work with that. I'm the MacGuyver of jerking off to things. Give me a flashlight, some yarn, a box of raisins and a tongue depressor and I'll figure out a way to fap to it.

For instance, remember that time we went Tijuana and saw the donkey show? I mean, I knew that chick was going to blow the Donkey, but I didn't know she was actually going to let it stick it's spongy, half-formed-looking phallus inside her asshole! Remember how afterwards she blasted shit and donkey cum halfway across the bar from her gaping asshole and a big chunk of her corn-laden scat flew into your mouth and you puked all over the guy next to you, causing half the bar to start fighting and the other half to start puking and before we knew it the whole floor was carpeted with puke and cum and shit and blood. I still managed to rub one out that night! I tell you. . . .

Wait. You're not the one that went with me to Tijuana, are you? Shit.

Awkward.

The Amazing Atheist,
July 29th, 2007

CHRISTIANS ARE STUPID, EVIL, CHILD-ABUSERS.

According to the Bible, God created the Earth in six days.

According to calculations by Charles Lineweaver and Daniel Grether at the University of New South Wales there are about 100 billion stars with planets in our Galaxy. That means that, with 100 billion galaxies in the known universe, there are *at least* 10 trillion planets out there.

Do you see where I'm going with this?

How did a God who took six days to create our pathetic little planet do the same trick 10 trillion times since then? It would have taken God 60 trillion days to create every planet in the universe. That's 164,383,561,643 years of worth work, give or take a few months.

From the genealogies found in the Bible, Christian 'scholars' have deduced that the Earth is between six and ten-thousand years old.

"Well," says the ever crafty fundie, "maybe God created those other planets first, to prepare the universe for us!"

Nice try, christsucker.

"In the beginning God created the Heaven and the Earth."
Genesis 1:1

"That doesn't prove anything!" further protests our missing link between man and tree stump, "It says he created the heaven first. The heaven could include those planets."

Heaven is a place of unending bliss, remember? If those planets were part of God's heaven, then going to Heaven would be as easy as building the *USS Enterprise*.

"Translation error!"

But . . .

"TRANSLATION ERROR! JESUS DIED FOR YOUR SINS!"

Ah, translation errors—the last refuge of a thoroughly defeated Christian. When you hear the words "translation error," pat yourself on the back. You've just won. Every argument with a fundamentalist Christian goes through six basic steps.

1. *Atheist challenges scripture.*

2. *Theist defends scripture.*

3. *Atheist refutes defense.*

4. *Theist makes statement about the glory of Christ and his dying for our sins.*

5. *Atheist continues to press original issue.*

6. *Theist claims a translation error.*

I don't recommend pressing the issue beyond step six for a reason that is exactly one word long: **Salem**. Don't think they'd hesitate to kill you. These are the same people who still support Bush and the war in Iraq. They have no moral qualms about purging the world of sinners.

In fact, they have no morals at all.

Nothing bears this out better than the psychological, and in many cases physical, torture that they inflict upon their own children. Let me ask you a question (You can't answer or argue! God, I love this medium!): Why the fuck is it legal to tell toddlers that they could go to Hell?

Don't get me wrong. There exist few bigger freedom fans than me. The first amendment to the constitution guarantees all people in the United States freedom of religion, without government interference. To my way of thinking, passing a law against teaching your children about your religion is unconstitutional. Aside from that, there is a limit to how much I am willing to meddle with the upbringing of any child. Most child-rearing decisions belong to parents, plain and simple.

However, children are not property. They are human beings who should be extended a certain degree of individual rights. Modern society does not allow parents to beat their children, despite the bible's endorsement of corporal punishment. While I don't necessarily agree that all spanking should be illegal, I think that the vast majority of people would agree that there is a line that should not be crossed. Parents do not have to right to mangle their children's bottoms (or any other part of them), regardless of what their holy texts might say about it. The action of beating one's children is illegal. Doing it in the name of God is no less illegal.

Now imagine the psychological abuse of being taught from an age before your reasoning faculties are developed, that if you do not obey the doctrines of a religion that you have no hope of understanding, you will burn in a pit of unfathomable torment where demons will gnaw at every centimeter of your flesh and the unimaginable heat of fire too hot to comprehend will drag multi-pronged dagger-tongues across your soul until the end of time. I see that as being worse than a beating in the long run. You might as well just hand the kid a rifle and point him to the nearest bell tower.

So, why do we allow it? I can't think of a good reason. We'd never allow a parent to tell their child, "If you don't obey me, I will pull out all of your teeth with an old pair of pliers and fuck your mouth!" so why do we allow, "If you don't obey God (me), you'll go to a land of eternal torment to writhe in agony for infinities upon infinities!"

If you remove the sacred cow status of religion for a moment and look at the situation objectively, I'm sure you won't be able to answer the following question.

Who does more damage to a child: a one-time rapist or a parent who teaches them that if they're not good they'll burn in hell forever?

Whatever your answer, I'm willing to bet that you actually had to stop to think about it.

CONVERSION COUNTER: 0 AND STEADY

I once remarked that converting a Christian to atheism is like changing the label on a jar of pickled dog turds. I stand by that statement.

Many Atheists give oblivious credence to the notion that an imbecilic theist will, once converted to atheism, transform into the most brilliant of brights, the most spectacular of secularists, the apotheosis of atheistic intellectual integrity—and other such corny alliterations. The sad truth is that a shit-for-brains who thinks that Papa Smurf in the sky is watching his every move with unwavering concern will, if converted (or deconverted, if you prefer) to atheism, become a shit-for-brains who thinks that books are a nifty decoration. You'll not improve such a person—if anything, you'll make him worse.

Consider, for a moment, Eric Harris and Dylan Klebold, the shooters at Columbine High School. They were as atheistic as I am, but they embraced the dogmatism of the thoroughly debunked idea of Social Darwinism (which should rightly be called Social Spencerism). They managed to convince themselves that their shootings were, in some way, natural selection. If they'd been Christians, they might have killed for Jesus. Instead, they were Atheists, and they killed for Nietzsche and Darwin. That's not progress by any definition of the word that I would embrace.

I WARN YOU FURTHER: In an atheist world, atheism will no longer be a badge of intellectual prowess. Those of you who revel in your elitism now may well find yourself clutching at straws to justify your worth in the secular utopia of your fondest dreams.

And who will we do intellectual battle with? Each other? I know we *say* that, but is it really what we desire? In your little black hearts can't you admit, if only to yourselves, that it's a lot more fun using your vast intellect to anally rape the cognitively deficient than it is rationally discussing ideas with your equals?

I suppose we can always argue with the social Darwinists—but as far as pseudo-science's created solely to justify the actions of the powerful against the powerless go, intelligent design will never be topped. It will always hold that special place in our hearts, won't it? Won't you look back on the pwnage of those imbeciles and smile? I know I will.

I imagine myself in the old atheist's home, sitting in my rocking chair, being blown by holographic teenagers while robot nurses pump apple-sauce down my throat through little grey tubes. Atop my nightstand I'll have a little scrapbook of all the believers I ever crushed in one-sided, totally unfair debates. I'll look at their pictures and I'll laugh myself to sleep each night, but inside I'll be crying.

Without religion, there is no religion to destroy. Our victory is our defeat.

ISLAM IS LAME

"YOU THINK YOU HAVE BALLS? I WOULD CHOP YOUR HEAD OFF YOU PATHETIC FAT SHIT. YOU ATHEIST BASTARDS HAVE DESTROYED THIS WORLD WITH YOUR EVOLUTION THEORY, SAYING LIFE IS MATTER OF CHANCE. THAT IS WHY THEIR IS DEPRESSION AND SUICIDE BECAUSE ATHEIST LIFE IS BASE ON PERFORMANCE. IF I MET YOU I WOULD DO ALLAH SWIFT HONOR AND THE UMMAH HONOR OF CHOPPING YOUR HEAD OFF AND DRAINING YOUR BLOOD! KEEP HIDING BEHIND YOUR COMPUTER! COME TO ENGLAND AND SAY THAT TO MY FACE AND I WILL STAB YOU UP, YOU PIG HONKY. LOL."

MuhammadFaysalNawa, Youtube User
(abysmal spelling and punctuation has been corrected)

"FUCK YOU, racist fucking kafir! I wish I could chop your fucking head off you fat fuck! Islam OWNS YOU, bitch!"

islamistic123, Youtube User
(abysmal spelling and punctuation has been corrected)

"Hey, man, why you are insulting Islam? This is a very big thing! You had better back off these shitty things or you are a dead man, I swear to God."

karimsaber123, Youtube User
(abysmal spelling and punctuation has been corrected)

HOW TO GET LEFT THE FUCK ALONE

I am vulgar. I think bad thoughts and more often then not I shit them forth from my mouth with all the enthusiasm of an overpaid whore on ecstasy. What's worse, I usually say them when in mixed company, or when speaking to one with fragile ears, and a frail mind in between them.

Jaws drop and gasps resound. "Did he really just say what I think he did?" You're damn right he did. And do you know what? He enjoyed it too. It's how I maintain my sanity, and now, with my help, you too can improve the quality of your life by being a dirty foul-mouthed bastard.

"*How can being grossly offensive improve my life, Amazing Atheist?*"

God you people ask some dumb fucking questions. Observe my ingenious equation below.

$$People + Life = \otimes$$

$$Life - People = \odot$$

And how do you get rid of people? You can stick dynamite in their asses and paint the walls with their insides . . . which is effective, but illegal and costly.

You can poison their coffee, but it tends to be slow—and problematic if they drink tea or water or cat piss.

The best solution to your people problem is to make your company utterly un-enjoyable by totally offending anyone foolish enough to seek your conversation.

"*How do I accomplish this feat, Amazing Atheist? I am not clever and witty like you.*"

I know. Don't fret. I'm here to help. There are four basic methods of fucking with peoples stupid heads.

1. The Grumbling Prick Method
2. The "My Life is Shit" Method.
3. The Polite Asshole Method

4. The Amazing Atheist Method

THE GRUMBLING PRICK METHOD

This method is usually effective on those who want to ask for favors or opinions, and best of all for you dumbfucks, it's so easy that it doesn't even require any brain activity. Basically, you just grumble.

Victim: "Hey, AA, can I borrow some salmon?"

Me: "Grrrrrrr . . . Flippidyskittlefucker! YOU KNOW NOT MY POWAH!!!"

Victim: "What?"

Me: "Fraggenrippert shitterpickfork eat nachos in hellzzor!!!"

Victim: "Uh. I'll come back later."

THE "MY LIFE IS SHIT" METHOD

This is the favorite among whiney people, who, for the most part, don't even understand that it repels people. Basically, when you are approached by an undesirable, you start whining about everything wrong in your life. If you have a relatively happy life, just make some shit up. The more inane the shit you bitch about, the better. If you bitch about valid things, then your misery is likely to be compelling—which you don't want. For instance:

Victim: "Hi, TJ!"

Me (in depressed voice): "Hi."

Victim: "Something the matter? You sound down."

Now, this is where you hit them with it. Your response should be inane and whiney. You don't want to compel them.

WRONG RESPONSE: "Oh. Nothing much. A serial killer murdered everyone I loved and brutally raped me."

That's sure to lead to a lot of consolation that you don't want.

RIGHT RESPONSE: "*Something* the matter? No. EVERYTHING is the matter. I've got a paper cut. My Coke is flat. My Toes hurt. My hands are kind of cold. And to top it all off, people that I hate keep trying to talk to me."

THE POLITE ASSHOLE METHOD

This method requires more brains than the others, and is the least effective in getting rid of people since many are too thick to even know that they are being insulted. However, this is the best method for those desiring a feeling of superiority to those that they are insulting. You most commonly see this technique used by people who want to insult people who are ridiculous, but have a lot of authority.

Basically, you insult them subtly, and make it sound like a compliment. A good sense of irony is needed for this one.

Victim: "Do you think that they will ever create a computer with Artificial Intelligence?"

Me: I don't think a machine could function on your intellectual level, sir.

Victim: Really?

Me: Oh yeah. A computer with a brain like yours wouldn't know what to do with itself.

THE AMAZING ATHEIST METHOD

This is my favorite method, and not just because it's named after me. I won't even bother explaining, because you'd never understand, but I'll give you an example:

Victim: "Hi, TJ, do you want to go swimming?"

Me: "In your bloody remains maybe."

Victim: "Um . . . huh?"

Me: "Fuck you, you shriveled scrotum sack!"

Victim: "Hey! Fuck you, uh . . . asshole!"

Me: "SUCK THE BALLS OF THE GREAT MONKEY DEMON!"

Victim: "Eeeeeeek!" (faints.)

"Wow, Amazing Atheist, you sure are the greatest genius to ever live." Yes. And you aren't even worthy of my great wisdom. Anyhow, I'm off to drink the urine of 17 virgin cattle so that I may unlock the secrets of the multiverse and all of its special juicy cosmic-type powers.

HOW TO WRITE A BOOK

This is what writers do. They sit down and write. You don't need a big vocabulary. Hell, you don't even have to have much of anything to say. Most things, after all, will say themselves if you let them.

Another thing to remember is that you have to write what you feel like writing; you'll never get anywhere if you write what you think. That's probably why I'm struggling so much with this medium. I'm not a very emotional person. Shit. If I even unlocked the feelings that I know must be somewhere deep inside me (probably near the crotch) I would be better than Shakespeare. Well, not really. But I could be pretty goddamned good—better than any of these fucking monkeys that are writing today.

That's kind of funny. Isn't that how it always starts? You look at the work of those who are getting paid for something and realize, *that's awful! I could do better than that!* And that's when the little light bulb manifests out of thin air right above your head. You realize that you've just found your calling. Writing! What could be better? You can remain as lazy as you ever were and never have to go out doors. You can be as ugly as a festering splatter of runny cat shit and still become an internationally recognized celebrity with infinite wealth.

Well, actually, most writers make next to nothing and have to hang on to their day jobs to pay the rent, but fuck those guys! You aren't going to be one of those! You're going to be a number one bestseller. Stephen King will beg to suck your dick so that he may achieve an inkling of your tremendous talent by stealing your semen and using it to make a clone of you so that he can steal its inevitably brilliant ideas. You could write a book about your right nut and sell more than J.K. Rowling. That is the extent of your talent.

After having had this epiphany, you rush home and break out the old typewriter (PC's are for pussies). After you get the dust out of every crevasse and yank the dead rat out of the roller, you're ready to begin work on your masterpiece. No ideas emerge immediately. You give up and go to sleep saying that you'll try it again tomorrow.

The next day you sit, gazing madly at the blank sheet of paper. After a few hours you type an 'M.' You stare it with the attentiveness of a coked-out president peeking in at one of his hot daughters showering through a cracked door (nothing against "good ol' G Dubbya." I ain't no terrorist-lover). What the fuck is wrong with that fucking M? He's just sitting there, looking at you in his smug, smart-ass way. FUCK HIM! You lift the typewriter up and toss it across the room right into your TV set, smashing the screen to smithereens. That's okay, you tell yourself, it is unbefitting a writer such as myself to watch television anyway.

You decide that the typewriter approach is outdated. You decide that you need to go buy a brand new PC. Unfortunately you have no way to pay for it unless you take all the money out the savings account that you've had since you were a little kid and would sell your body to the local sex offender. That's okay though, you're going to be a filthy stinking-ass rich writer soon. You'll show that fucking M! You'll never put him in any of your stories! There wont be any M's in your stories! No sir!

On your way out the door your phone rings. You pick it up. It's your boss wondering where you were all day. You tell him to go fuck himself up the ass with a big, floppy, rubber dick. You hang up the phone and giggle at your cleverness. You feel better all ready.

A few hours later, you're back with your brand new, deluxe, limited addition XK-33 with an ultimum 666 processor and a flat-screen monitor. The side of the box reads, THE OFFICIAL COMPUTER OF SATAN. You smile and nod with self-approval at you excellent purchase. You bring it into your work room (formerly called the bathroom) and plug that bad boy in. It explodes into flames and burns down your apartment complex, killing two and injury twenty. You are badly burned, but the paramedics tell you that your insurance has expired.

No biggie! The burns don't hurt that much, and you're sure you can sleep at a friend's house until you get back on your feet. And tomorrow you can go back to that computer shop and give them Hell! You hop in your car. It won't start. Who cares? It's a nice night for walking anyway.

After a few hours (during which you could not locate one working payphone) you arrive at your friend apartment. He is not home. You begin to feel a bit angry and decide to mutilate the first person you see. You spot and old granny walking her tiny poodle around the block. The bitch must die! You run after her screaming obscenities at the top of your lungs. Her face contorts in panic and she grabs a Glock .9mm out of her purse. You scream, jump back and try to run, but granny isn't having it!

"Thought you could off me, huh? Ya sonuvabitch!" she yells passionately, while unloading two bullets into you—one in each butt cheek. You fall to the ground and turn on your side. She uses this opportunity to kick your nuts a few times. Then, as you clutch them in pain, her dog mistakes your face for a fire-hydrant. After she leaves, you lie there and pray for death. It doesn't come, but the police do.

They arrest you, but it's not such a bad thing. At least you'll get some medical attention, and you'll have plenty of time to write in prison.

HOW TO SEEM SMART

Even though you will, over the course of my numerous lessons, become much smarter than you are now, you'll still be fairly stupid. Which is okay, since advancement in human society is based not on how intelligent you are, but how intelligent you can seem to those handing out social promotions.

"I don't understand, Amazing Atheist! BLaaaaaarrGGGHH! Why come is I be so dumb?"

It's okay. I'll simplify it for you:

You are stupid. The Amazing Atheist is smart. But if you follow his instructions to a T you can at least *seem* smart to others. Thus, your position in the social hierarchy will rise faster than your dick at the sight of any sort of farm animal.

VOCABULARY

A timeless method for seeming smarter than you could ever hope to be is to use incredibly complicated language to communicate any task. For example:

Concise Language: "My friends and I will go to the store and get some food."

'Genius' Language: "Presently, myself and some acquaintances shall embark upon a journey to the local market in the pursuit of reasonably priced sustenance to sate our appetites in the immediate and for a period of days forthcoming."

Sure, people won't understand what you're saying, but you'll seem smart to them because you used lots of really big words. This is because they, like you, are stupid and have no concept as to what actually constitutes intelligence.

SILENCE

Abraham Lincoln once said, "It is better to keep your mouth shut and be thought a fool than to open it up and get your tongue eaten by evil flies."

Or something along those lines.

Anyhow, the point is this: **shut the fuck up.** For some reason, people who don't talk much are considered to be intelligent. Perhaps because it is assumed that they are deep in thought about physics or genetic enhancement of the male sexual organ, or whatever it is that smart people think about.*

GLASSES
Smart people wear glasses. This is a well known fact among anyone who watches TV. If a guy (or gal) wears glasses, let it be known that they are probably capable of building atom bombs using only duct tape and silly putty. If you already wear glasses, great. If you don't, go get some. It is a good idea to get the ugliest possible pair in the store since everyone knows that smart people have no . . .

FASHION SENSE
BACK AWAY FROM THE DESIGNER BRANDS! From now on you shop at K-mart, where you will buy only the most repulsive clothes that you can find. You need stuff that positively screams, "I AM A GEEK! I'M TOO SMART TO WASTE TIME DRESSING MYSELF LIKE A HUMAN BEING." If you have trouble finding clothes that scream that, record it on a pocket recorder and play it in a continuous loop everywhere you go.

THE LAUGH
Smart people do not laugh the same way, or at the same things, that other people do. You must perfect a laugh that sounds something like a bat getting butt-fucked by and elephant. This will take time and practice, and I recommend that you allow yourself to get butt-fucked by an elephant (just once) so that you can get in the proper frame of mind. You don't have to, I suppose. If you do, be sure to take pictures and send them to all the members of your family as well as your classmates/co-workers. Smart people are always doing eccentric things like

that, and you will notice a big change in the way people view you.

But, I digress.

Another important factor is what you laugh at. Things that you find funny now, like *Big Momma's House 2*, just aren't gonna cut it in the intellectual community. Watch Monty Python and just laugh every time it seems like there was a joke. Eventually you will begin to think that you actually understand the humor and will be able to pick up on smart people jokes in the real world.

"But what happens when I have to tell a joke of my own, Amazing Atheist? Won't it reveal to them my overwhelming stupidity?"

Nah. Smart people are fairly slow to pick up on things like that. Their minds are always analyzing things. If you tell a joke that hints your stupidity, just laugh and say, "I don't know what came over me. I apologize for my immaturity." Then start bitching about Bill Gates, or an upcoming sci-fi or fantasy film. This will divert their minds from your digression from established intellectual standards of humor.

*For those of you wondering, the thing that smart people actually do think about most is how unfair it is that they are trapped on a planet full of imbeciles.

HOW TO PWN MY ASS ON YOUTUBE

Despite frequent attempts from a plethora of sources, ranging from Encyclopedia Dramatica to Jordi Cruise, I have yet to feel truly pwned here on "the internets." Hopefully, this helpful pwnage guide will change this fact forever.

SEIZE MY INSECURITIES

You'll make no progress simply calling me fat. If I were sensitive about my weight, don't you think I'd make a better attempt to conceal it?

If you really want to get to me, point out words that I mispronounced or logical fallacies within my arguments. If I misspelled a word in my title or description, jump on it like CapnOAwesome jumps on an opportunity to whore himself out for even the faintest possibility of a new subscriber. There's nothing I hate worse than feeling stupid.

UNCOVER MY CONTRADICTIONS

I have plenty of contradictions from video to video. I leave them up because I assume that no one will ever be anal retentive enough to notice them. Prove me wrong. Find two clips of me saying totally contradictory things and play them side by side to make me look like a jackass who doesn't know what he's talking about.

WHEN ALL ELSE FAILS, POINT OUT MY FAILINGS

People seem to adore pointing out my shortcomings rather than arguing with my position. So, for my beloved collection of invective-spewing haters, I submit this bullet-point list of some of my failings.

- My oral hygiene is below average (above average in Britain).
- I neglect my toenails. They're quite ugly.
- I pick my nose to an obscene amount and examine my finds afterwards.
- I waft my own farts upwards so that I can catch their

aroma.
- I play with my balls for at least one hour each day.
- And smell my hands afterwards.
- I have masturbated to "The Simpsons."
- My penis is small enough to fit in your pocket. Twice.
- I fantasize about being cooked alive by sexy female cannibals.
- I masturbate to deviant pornography.
- When I was 11, I shit in the cat litter box just to see what it would feel like.
- My nose is covered in black heads that I've made no attempt to treat.
- Because of my fair skin and massive fatness, I have revolting stretch marks up and down both sides of my body.
- I have back hair.
- I wear the same pair of jeans for weeks because I'm too lazy to transfer my things from one pocket to the next.
- I keep arguing a point even after I've been proven wrong because I'm too embarrassed to admit defeat.

EVERYTHING'S FINE

According to the right, the world is about to end. We have sinned against God and soon his judgment will be upon us and everyone (except those brought up to Heaven in the rapture) will suffer horribly. Liberal extremists will conquer the planet, gay orgies will spread like wildfire, and abortions will become as commonplace as brushing your teeth (this may be a bad example for those of you living in Great Britain). The only answer is to mandate prayer in schools, burn the Bill of Rights and, for the love of all that is holy, stop teaching children that evolution nonsense!

According to the left, the world is about to end. We have sinned against mother nature and soon the ice caps will melt and everyone will suffer horribly. Greedy multi-national corporations will conquer the planet until every last human being on earth works for slave wages. The only answer is to stop eating meat, drive hybrid cars and stop saying anything even remotely offensive about anyone other than George W. Bush.

I have a question.

Doesn't anyone else think that things are fine and that we're all being arrogant and reactionary? When the Earth starts getting warmer, we say, "Must be something we did!" and ignore any evidence to the contrary. It sounds right to the left on a visceral level. We're so important that it must be our fault! Look, I'm the last person to argue with scientists, but climate science is one of the trickiest branches there is. Meteorologists can't figure out the weekly forecast half the time, but Climatologists are 100% certain that human CO_2 levels are responsible for global warming? From a purely common sense standpoint, it just doesn't sound very reasonable.

Climate scientists are quick to point out that the earth is, "as hot as it's been in 12,000 years," but this planet is 4.5 billion years old. If it was this hot as recently as 12,000 years ago, then why is it so unusual that it's this hot now? The fact is that, just a million years ago, the Earth's climate was completely different than it is now. The sea level was 80 feet higher. The air was far more humid and stifling. Imagine planet Louisiana. It got from there to here without our help. Why do we automatically assume that it must be our fault that it's going back again?

Sure, adjusting to a changing climate will suck, but that's what evolution is for—adapting. And if the planet becomes uninhabitable, that would certainly suck but we've already got caffeinated donuts and Die Hard 4 . . . I think it's safe to say that we've had a good run.

The conservative's arguments for what's wrong in the world makes even less sense. At least liberals have the scientific community behind their doomsday scenario. The neocons have only got "biblical" evidence (read: jack shit).

And the conservative idea of hell on earth is rampant alternative sex and drugs with no legal consequences whatsoever. If this hell were ever realized, people like me would find themselves in heaven.

Meanwhile, their idea of heaven—you know, clouds and harps and all that jazz, er, gospel—is about the least appealing thing in the world to anyone with half a brain and a set of balls (don't be offended ladies, the analogy could as easily be 'and a functional cunt') It would be like the worst hell imaginable! Eternal bliss may sound good to the people who have never even had a single second of bliss in their lives, but those of us who have orgasmed without procreation even crossing our minds and not felt so much as a single iota of guilt afterwards, know that there is little worse in life (or afterlife, I'd presume) than too much of a good thing.

For the sake of making a larger point, let's all pretend that the conservative notion of human liberty as the apotheosis of immorality is, indeed, as bad as they think it is. Let's just ask ourselves these two questions:

Could the liberals be right about the world being fucked by global warming?

Could the conservatives be right about the world being fucked by God?

The respective answers are maybe and no.
	But the more important question here is, "what about the people who think things are the best they've ever been and are getting better?" We exist, I assure you. Don't we get a say in all this? Where's our media exposure? Where are our celebrity icons? Our propaganda films?
	All we've really got is that stupid fucking Bobby McFerrin song, "Don't Worry, Be Happy." But how can we not worry when everyone else assures us that there's so many things that we need to worry about? How can we be happy in a world full of miserable people?
	Being an optimist sucks.

THE OUTSIDER GENERATION

In all my years of spouting my crazy opinions, I have no recollection—not one—of ever changing anyone's mind about anything.

I've written essays and poems and songs and stories and paragraph-long insanities on a million different subjects, but none of it has ever made anyone who didn't already agree with me say, "Wow, you're right!" I've constructed arguments that I believed to be air-tight, but my enemies keep breathing comfortably. I've produced, on a few occasions, nearly incontrovertible evidence to back up this claim or that claim, but the dissenters only scowled at me and stayed their course.

As I've stayed mine.

I state my opinion, you state yours—and neither of us changes our mind? Neither of us improves or evolves in any immediately conceivable way?

No one wants to change their mind about anything. They actively resist it. They hate the very notion of it. If you examine the words "change your mind" closely, with a psychologist's eye, it's easy to see the source of these fears.

Hell, if there was ever a word that scared the living pig shit out of every man walking this little ball of shit in our toilet bowl of a galaxy, its change:

"Things change," says the scraggly villain when the hero falls.

"You've changed," says your girl or boyfriend just before they dump you.

"He's changing!" screams the protagonist of a werewolf story when someone begins the transformation.

It's a very negative word. At least, usually. It does have positive connotations as well:

"It's time for a change," says a new leader to a crowd sick of the way their old leader mislead them.

"Nothing ever changes," someone says sadly. (This is a negative statement, but change has positive connotations.)

The rule here is easy enough to discern—change has a positive connotations in dissatisfactory circumstances and a negative connotations when people are content (or content enough) with the way things are.

So when someone tries to change your mind, you reject their attempts. Why? Because you're a human being who secretly believes that you are perfect, in spite of your character flaws, of which you are mostly aware. You are content enough in your mind to feel as though it is untouchable and sacred—something to be preserved at all costs.

Why do you think the first step any cult leader or government agent takes to brainwash someone involves eroding their sense of identity and smashing their self-esteem to pieces?

Any human being functioning normally is not very susceptible to the overt suggestions of his fellow man, despite our instinct to take cues from the pack and go along with whatever the general consensus is. In fact, ironically enough, our built in conformity streak is a big part of what makes us so reluctant to go along with people. This is because we are "wired" to distrust the outsider and accept only the ideas of those within our social group. In this age of extremely limited social interaction, this mechanism, once crucial to the evolutionary process, has begun to destroy us.

People are cynics who distrust everything. In the 1950's when the government and corporations churned out endless propaganda, the masses, for the most part, believed every word of it. Today, people distrust everything they hear, everything they read, everything they see, everyone they meet. Nearly a fourth of people believe that the Government was responsible for the attacks of September 11th.

I suspect that people have always been terribly jittery creatures, a race of idiots recoiling from their own shadows, but there was always an "us" and a "them." Us was a collective of individuals that could be trusted—they go to the same church as you, the have the same values as you, **they are you**.

Them was any one that belonged to any other group and believed a slew on unwholesome, terrible things.

Now there is no us. There is only them.

We are a generation born to belong nowhere, a generation charged with making out own clique, but we don't want to. And what is to blame for our reluctance? The conformist mechanism, that component of our psyche that tells us that we're not to trust outsiders—but now everyone is an outsider.

We do not function as a group. We do not have a common ideology. We do not have a common system of values. We run the gamut.

Is this a good thing? Can anyone hope to compete with other social organisms when they haven't one of their own? Doesn't anyone want to get together and march to war with me?

Hell yes, you say?
But you want to lead?
Fuck that.
Never mind.

RAPE SURVIVOR
CHATROOM SURVIVOR

Rape isn't fatal.

So imagine my indignation when I saw a chatroom called "Rape Survivors." Is this supposed to impress me? Someone fucked you when you didn't want to be fucked and you're amazed that you survived? Unless he used a chainsaw instead of his dick, what's the big deal?

I don't mean to be horrendously offensive and insensitive here, but everyone survives rape. Some women are killed afterwards, but that's murder, not rape. To say that you're a rape survivor is as meaningless as saying you're a jury duty survivor or a divorce survivor. Lots of things in life suck—that doesn't mean we survived them.

The word survivor applies to people who are alive after being stabbed 73 times with an ice pick or mauled by rabid wolverines, not to a woman who gets dick when she doesn't want it. Just because you got raped, you have to rape the English language? You vindictive bitch!

Also, don't you ever get tired of being the victim? How many failed relationships are you going to blame on a single violation of your personal space? I'm not making light of it. I know that it is damaging, a reminder of your powerlessness against the world—but it should be a wake up call. We are all powerless against the forces of fate (or chance). We're all on different paths, but they all lead to the same place.

Life leaves no survivors.

NOTE ON THE ABOVE: I just showed this writing to a friend of mine, along with the question, "Is this too offensive to release?" I was looking for a yes. I got one. So, I've included it here. I'm here to cross lines. This is not The Amazing Atheist from those cute little youtube videos you love so much—this is the real me. And the real me doesn't give a fuck about your small-minded boundaries.

If you've been raped, does the above passage add insult to injury? Does it make it hurt worse? How could it? If rape is the paramount psychological trauma in life, then how could my words aggravate it whatsoever? Too often in this culture, we fear words. But even if my words are the height of ignorance, they should elevate you. If you find them funny, then you will laugh and dismiss them as a joke. If you find them honest, you will respect my bravery. If you find them infuriating, I will have given you power. If you find them sad, then I have enriched you.

Words never make less of a person, unless they are bland. If you feel something, then I've done my job as a writer.

SOMETHING HUMAN IN THE INHUMAN

I am a 35 year old mother of 4 sometimes in online chats. I have a 13-year-old daughter and men tell me how they want to rape her and I tell them how wet it makes my plump MILF pussy to hear them say that. Sometimes I meet men who go beyond that, who say they want to chop her young tits from her body, strangle her with a jump rope, things of that nature. My favorite scenario anyone ever conceived of was removing the jaws of all my children (the youngest of when I claimed to be 8) so that they would have direct access to their throats.

Other times I'm a strict father with two teenage daughters. People write to me, asking for explicit details regarding their spankings, offering hints as to what they want to here. For instance, the question, "Do you make them get naked for spankings?" should always be answered yes.

Sometimes I'm a 20-year-old girl named Kara who wants to sell myself into slavery. Men tell me how they want to whip me frequently, make me keep a buttplug in 24 hours a day, force me to drink their piss and eat their shit, eventually snuffing me on camera for the whole world's pleasure.

How do the preceding paragraphs make you feel? Offended? Excited? Amused? Depressed?

I feel all of those things at once. I am offended that no one online ever rebukes me my perversity, but that they instead actually revel in it. I'm excited by how many perverts like me there are in the world. I'm amused because I know that, like me, they're all talk and no action. I'm depressed because I wish I had it in me to be all action and no talk.

Internet sex chats are where people go to lie to one another about what they're capable of; pageants of lustful deceit where sick fucks like myself go to keep our sicknesses from destroying us. Zoophiles, pedophiles, slaves, masters, cannibalism fetishists, sadists, masochists—monsters of all shapes, sizes and colors congregating in a judgment-free environment for the purpose of helping each other get off. It's a beautiful thing, really.

Ted, the overweight divorced accountant from Virginia becomes Ted, the tall, muscular polygamist with seven curvy wives that he slaps around for his amusement and 12 daughters that he molests on the side. I talk to him as Debbie, the luscious and naive 19-year-old that's looking to become wife number 8. We both know that we're being deceived, and we don't care. We're telling lies to each other and stroking our cocks all the while.

Ted and I have made a connection. A real one. Sure, it's based on deception, but it's a mutual deception, a deception that we have both consented to. I jerk off to your lies, you jerk off to mine. That's what scientists call a symbiotic relationship.

It's amazing how, in a world where people are so disconnected from one another, some of us can find true and meaningful (I'm tempted to say "loving") connection in the most unlikely of places.

You can rape my daughter if you want. Sure, I don't have a daughter and if I did there's no way in hell I'd let you so much as *glance* at her, but in this consequence free environment, feel free to exercise your demons on her. Slit her throat and fuck the wound if you want to. It doesn't matter.

I'm not judging you. I'm jerking you.

IT'S SMALL.
GET OVER IT.

People always feel the need to defend my penis from me, even when I'm not attacking it. All I have to do is mention that it is small and people will say, "I'm sure it's just fine."

"I didn't say it wasn't fine. I just said it was small."

"It's not small, I'm sure."

"No," I insist, puzzled that they would argue with me about a piece of my anatomy, "It is."

"It probably just looks small because you're such a big guy."

"Well, that probably makes it look smaller, but even disregarding that, it's small."

"Why are you so down on yourself?" they ask.

"I'm not," I always explain at that point. "I don't have anything against my penis, but the fact is that it is a small penis. Any shame I might have about that I lost after getting laid a few times and realizing that it wasn't the end of the world."

A girl told me a story once. She told me that she was once lying naked in bed, legs spread apart, waiting for some guy she had just met to come in and fuck her. He entered the room, looked down at her, and started undressing. But at that last crucial moment, the revelation of what he was packing, he unveiled a miniscule member, probably roughly the size of mine, and she closed her legs instantly and left him standing there to wallow in his woe.

I told her, "You're lucky it wasn't me. I'd have busted your fucking nose."

So maybe I am still a little sensitive about it.

But hey, it's easier to convince chicks to do anal.

ILL LOGIC

I am not easily bored. I'm very content with tranquility, because my mind is a circus freak show of deformed demons and holy holes. I can sit for hours in what is perceived as aloofness, when in reality, or rather, out of reality, I am moving at a million miles a second, reveling in my genius and lamenting my idiocy. I sit there with a blank expression on my face—the world scarcely pays attention. They have no idea that I am in another place; a place where the beauty of ugliness is understood completely and so am I. In this wonderful, horrible world, I am an all-powerful god, whose every perversion is immediately fulfilled. I reign over the populace like the eidolon named night from Edgar Allen Poe's poem, *Dream-land*. I suppose that is exactly what the world of my thoughts is: a dream-land.

The real world finds me in an infinitely less enjoyable position. I am a spineless coward, insecure in myself and unable to muster the will to take any step towards improving the quality of my existence. Despite the fact that I am blessed with luxuries that most don't have, I am apathetic. Even in the face of adversity, I remain unfazed and uncaring. I neglect my hygiene to the point of disgusting those around me. I am infatuated with a pathetic fantasy world that is obviously a product of my shallow, meaningless life. Dream-land is basically a necessary antithesis of reality—artificial flavoring if you will.

I take some (but not much) comfort in the knowledge that I am at least intelligent enough to analyze and understand my delusions. That is supposed to be the mark of a true philosopher: the ability to analyze ones own delusions. It is for this reason that I have chosen to write this. I feel that we live in times that are in need of a new philosopher; someone who realizes both his inadequacy and his greatness; his kindness and his cruelty; his love and his lust. That someone is me—or it isn't. Only my time and your ridicule will tell.

It is amazing how many people can formulate a

rationale to justify their actions or further their cause. Obviously, logic is not flawless. It is, in all honesty, very flawed. Different minds make different connections and have different prejudices; therefore we are inclined to side with the rationale that best rewards us. We will actively and consciously defy what we know to be true in order to obtain our ideal. But what, if anything, do we know to be true? Well, according to Descartes, we only truly know in the existence of ourselves as a conscious stream of thought. Sadly, it is the true nature of this thought stream that is so often raped and mutilated by institutions such as religion, politics and the education system.

But if logic is flawed, how is one supposed to advance an argument?

It is a question that is probably bubbling in your mind right now. The answer is simple enough—one can't.

So then, why bother to attack logic in the first place?

Because far too many people have forgotten that logic can be imperfect. It should seem obvious, when there are so many contradicting ideas out there, but it has become so blatant and common that it is rarely ever perceived anymore. I want all who read this to realize that logic is not natural law, and we have no standardized system of it. The truth is that logic is a blunt force instrument, used as a weapon or a shield for institutions that have no true merit.

Religion- Pious logic is the most dangerous and flawed of all the forms of logic. It is logic that only makes sense if one is willing to blindly accept the unprovable as fact. In the case of Christianity, all that is required is a belief in God. Christian logic states that God created the universe and knows and sees all things. Therefore, his opinions are automatic facts. His opinions, as well as his guidelines for living, are all collected in a book entitled *The Holy Bible*. So, it can be logically assumed that *The Bible* is always right and any other logic is just the flawed logic of man. This only works, however, if you believe in God. But when you try to rationalize the existence of God, you end up with the following paradox: Christians believe in God because *The Bible* told them to, and they believe in *The Bible* because God told them to. Atheists like myself are all too familiar with this circular reasoning.

Politics- Political logic is too often based upon something that is initially just propaganda. A clever politician knows how to confuse even the most intelligent of people, simply by hiding the lack of substance behind a wall of euphemous logic. All the rationality in the world means nothing if it is built upon a foundation of nothingness.

Advertising- If you drink beer, beautiful women will want to have sex with you. If you have any problem spotting the flaw in that logic, then you need to go take some cyanide, because you're a waste of existence.

Law- Justice System logic is reliant on the infallibility of the justice system. That is all the justification they feel they need. Any logic beyond that point is simply for decorative purposes. Example: prostitution is illegal, but as comedian George Carlin has often pointed out, it makes little sense for there to be a law against selling a thing which is legal to give away.

Notice a trend? Sound reasoning is often corrupted by extremely illogical suppositions at the foundational level. I suggest that you be extremely careful when considering a new idea. Always check the building material used for the foundation on which any rationale is based. But be wary, for distortions don't always occur at the foundation.

KEEP IN MIND- Even though I try to base all my logic on fact (or at least well thought out opinion), I am human, and just as liable to make an error in rationality as anyone. Do not consider anything I say through out the course of this book as being anything more than one man's thoughts and ideas. I hope that my ideas will feed your own, just as all of your ideas have fed mine. We must share knowledge and opinion with one another for as long as we are able. We may get our Nietzschian Ubermensche yet. It could be you.

THE GOD(DESS) SPEAKS

Say this unto the world of man.

This is the word of the god(dess) called dull throbbing as transcribed by the servant of reality and unreality—which are one in the same—Terroja.

I have given him his name to celebrate his significance and expose naked his irrelevance.

He is a living martyr . . . thus, he is a contradiction. Thus, an apt (anti)prophet for this age.

I do not exist. I am a figment of his imagination.

I exist. I am an imagination of his universe, which has an effect upon this larger universe—the mind of the one true God.

But let us not concern ourselves with Him. He is too important to be relevant. He is concerned with His own gods, and they with theirs.

Acknowledge the limitations of infinity.

Embrace the vastness of personal destiny.

An endless field of reflection, as a man standing between two giant mirrors will see an army of clones of himself—so are the gods of mortals. Every god is a mortal. Every mortal is a god.

The hierarchy is endless. Thus, position is irrelevant. You are the slave to, and master of, infinity.

Do not fear or fret if you fail to grasp this concept. Understanding is given sparingly.

Do not shun what your mind does not grasp. Perhaps heart or soul will be quicker to understand.

Mind=The universe. Your personal dull throbbing. I am mind.

Heart=If your mind is the universe, then your heart is the eye that views it and interprets its meaning.

Soul=Your soul is a string. Strings hold all things.

How can it be known that this is truth? It cannot. But the truth is what it wants to be to who wants it to be.

You demand concrete. Yet, you are given paper mache.

But in building a statue, which would you prefer?

If you seek ease, you will demand the paper mache.

If you seek longevity, you will demand the concrete.

Concrete statues crumble. You demand metal.

Metal will rust.

Nothing is eternal, save for existence itself, growing and changing.

"Sophistry!" you say. I try to sell you the flawed.

Yes and no. I give you what you want. And that is the only truth that you will ever accept.

How can you discriminate when you only accept what sounds good to you?

The rational man says, "I do not believe this."

The rational man ignores a heart and soul that beg aloud in his mind for him to accept the burden of true multireality—which is both reality and unreality. Or, if you prefer, perception and imagination.

Thus, he that embraces only concretions is no more rational than he who embraces only abstractions.

Wisdom lies not in choosing one or the other, but in recognizing the place of both.

OBSERVATIONS, INTROSPECTIONS & APHORISMS

LOVE AND HATE—It's easy to hate. It's fun to hate. It's comforting, like the buzz from a few pints of ale. It courses through your veins, throbbing, reassuring you or your superiority. When you hate a man, it's easy to watch him die. When you hate a cause, it's funny to see that cause fail. When you hate yourself—truly despise your every breath—there's nothing that can stand in your way.

It's hard to love. It's miserable to be in love or to love a thing. It's stifling, like smoke in the air. It courses through your veins, making you feel small and useless. When you love a person, it's easy for them to stab you in the back. When you love a cause, it's easy for that cause to consume you. When you love yourself—truly adore your every breath—you have everything to lose.

BEAUTY—*I am the dirt streaked against your windshield, stretched thin, cracked, ugly—but the light shines through me.*

I've never seen anything breath-taking. I've never had a moment in my life where my breath was stopped by the sheer perfection of a sight. I've known the intensity of fear, of hate, of self-loathing—but never beauty.

Everything that's supposed to be lovely is offset by the ugliness of my heart. How could I, who lies and hurts at every juncture, look at the beauty of a sunset and feel anything but wretched? The light of beauty only serves to illuminate my emptiness.

I would like to watch a city burn to the ground from a nearby hillside, huge flames reaching from the buildings to the sky, blotting out the stars with their smoke. That would take my breath away. That would make me feel alive.

What does that say about me?

PERFECTION—Being perfect is just another imperfection.

GREAT MEN—More great men have died than have ever lived.

INTERNET CELEBRITY IS A FATE WORSE THAN HELL

When I was 15, I would have done anything for even the smallest taste of fame, but now that I've had the smallest taste of fame I'd castrate myself with a toothpick before wanting even one more subscriber to my Youtube channel.

Imagine the stupidest, most annoying person you've ever met. Now imagine that person being annoyed to death by the people who write me letters everyday. I get about 10 to 20 private messages on youtube per day and they fit into four basic categories.

1. Horrifying.
2. Revolting.
3. Sickening.
4. "There's no way this is a real person"

The sentence **"amacing athiest u fucken rock"** is the most horrible thing I have ever seen. How could anyone who enjoys my videos be so fucking stupid? I'd rather have one million of the most vitriolic invective-spewing detractors than even one stupid fan. You're writing to me, yet you can't spell my name? How is that even fucking possible? You had to type my name to send me the message, so you must know how to spell it or it never would have reached me!

You fucking people are *mud*—made of dirt and piss.

I WANT TO KILL MYSELF
WHEN I GROW UP

Hunter S. Thompson blew his brains out on my birthday, which is also Kurt Cobain's birthday. It's odd, because sometimes I feel like I'm somewhere in between the two—part brooding loner, part raging truth-seeker. My writing lacks the fire of Thompson's, and it lacks the poetry and irony of Cobain's, but it's naked and self-revealing in the same way theirs were. I feel like I'm the heir to that throne sometimes—the suicide genius, the man who loves the whole world by hating himself.

Can one declare them self such a thing, or is that for the people to decide? I'd hate to think that it's in the hands of such a small-minded bunch of miserable cretins. But, the idea that it's in my hands is even worse in many ways.

This is such livejournal shit. I bet you feel stupid for paying 20 dollars for this. Fucking idiots!

Eh, cheer up! It's all good, right? What the fuck does it matter in the long run? We're all just biding our time until the day we become corpses. Everything we do from the cradle forth is just a distraction from the grave, a way of denying how fragile our lives are, how death is getting nearer and nearer.

It's a cruelty of nature that a being should have to understand the concept of death. We have so long fought against it with fanciful notions of an afterlife that is far better than our small lives here on earth. "This is all you get," are the most hopeless words that could ever be spoken in the ears of most people.

Death is not "far away." It isn't "just a transition." It's close, and it's forever.

In Defense Of Evil
Why *Good Is Bad and Bad Is Good*

By Terroja Kincaid

"Woe unto them that call evil good, and good evil"
-Isaiah 5:20

"Good is the thing that you favor. Evil is your sour flavor."
-Marilyn Manson

This book is dedicated to the scum of the earth who are tired of putting up with bullshit and aren't going to fucking take it one goddamn motherfucking second longer.

This book is also a greasy middle-finger waving in the face of every motherfucker who won't let you say "motherfucker" because they know that if they let you express yourself freely you'd show them for the lying cowardly fascist pig-fuckers that they are.

Finally, this book is dedicated to my Mom & Dad, who were fucked up enough to keep me from being one of the assholes described in the paragraph above but not so fucked up that they turned me into someone truly evil.

Evil, by its very definition, is indefensible. For this reason, the smarter among my readers may have guessed at the offset that this book's title is misleading. You will find no defenses of *actual* evil within this text. To attempt to justify the genocide of Adolf Hitler or the murder spree of The Zodiac Killer would be an exercise in callous anti-humanism, which does not interest me.

I have never been given to feelings of hatred towards my species as a whole. I look upon my fellow man not with loathing, but with bitter disappointment and a profound sense of detachment. I see these creatures called humans as uptight and humorless drones, bent on consumption, comfort and simplicity. Most are feeble, both intellectually and emotionally, unable to state their desires in simple terms, unable to pursue their wants in a responsible fashion, unable to treat each other with dignity in the face of disagreement.

For these and other reasons, I long ago seceded from the human race. I now comment on your species as an outsider, one removed from the struggles of your day to day lives by the simple act of not considering myself a part of your world.

This is not to say that I am without a stake in the human saga, but I am no more attached to you and your world than I am to the characters from my favorite films and books. It doesn't matter one iota to me that those characters are fictional and you are real. I am not prejudiced against good or interesting people simply because they don't necessarily "exist" in the traditional sense of the word.

Few of us are ever tested in the way that fictional characters often are. There are moments in all great fiction wherein the resolve of the protagonist is put to trial before a gauntlet of seemingly insurmountable obstacles. In surviving these obstacles, we learn the true character of our hero. We learn his strengths and weaknesses. We learn his values.

In real life, we know little of the true values of our fellow men and women. We know only what they espouse as their values. Further, we have too much of a stake in this world to see things clearly. Often, if a person betrays us, we determine them to be of poor character—but perhaps there are many instances where if we pulled back and looked at their situations more objectively, we'd discover that their motives for betraying us were good. Sadly, the worm can never be objective about the dietary needs of the early bird.

Similarly, I cannot look at my own species with objectivity unless I choose to secede from it. Thus my motives for abandoning my humanity are not solely the result of a dark impulse to become inhuman, but a trade-off, a deal with the devil. I still take delight in human triumph, just as I feel sorrow in human failing. I do not, however, take any credit or blame for either.

Perhaps some people will find this position to be little more than apathy with a patina of pseudo-Nietzschian rhetoric painted over it. It is not my intention to refute those people here. I would only ask that they keep their gavel from banging out the final verdict on my character until they've absorbed every word of this book. If they find me or my ideas wanting after they've turned the final page, then they can tell me so and I will smile and bear their maltreatment with all the poise I can muster. It will be easy, because no matter how you feel about this book or about me, the fact that you are reading these words means that I have your money. And make no mistake, ladies and gentleman, I will spend it frivolously.

Now that I've put my feelings regarding my relationship to my species into perspective, I can move forward with my explanation as to this book's title: *"In Defense Of Evil: Why Good Is Bad and Bad Is Good."* As I said before, it is not my intention to argue in favor of the genuine evils that man has displayed or to argue against man's true virtues.

This book is, instead, a criticism of false morality—false morality being defined as morality which serves no practical purpose for 21st century human beings, yet persists through the dubious methods of preservation employed by its proponents. Throughout this book I will provide examples of false morals and why they are impractical and often, when logic is applied to them, unethical. I will also show how many of the things that modern people overwhelmingly believe to be evil (even if many people shy away from that word itself) are in fact harmless or even positive.

In essence, the goal of this book is to show how modern

morality is a complete farce. I should state, for the terminally serious, that I have a rare condition known as a sense of humor that leads me to say things that I may not genuinely believe solely to amuse myself. If you find yourself getting irate and incensed by a particular passage, please be mindful of my increasingly rare condition and forgive me in advance.

Whence Cometh Evil?

Cody Weber's hair was blond the week that I went to visit him in the dirty little Midwest town of Keokuk, Iowa. He shoveled eggs into his mouth under the harsh light of the truckstop diner, talking, often with his mouth full, about his favorite subject: failure.

He spoke of how he was destined to be someone greater than the pallid lad sitting before me. He told me that as a child everyone had expected wondrous feats from him, had imagined him as a world conquering go-getter. This he spoke with sorrow.

When he came to the part where their fantasies of his all crumbled to the dust of disappointment, however, the pride in his voice was unmistakable.

Failure, for him, had been no accident. It had been an accomplishment—his defiant middle-finger to the tyranny of his own expected greatness.

It occurred to me, listening to him with what I imagine was a bemused grin, that we all craft a narrative for ourselves. We give our lives all the trimmings of a myth and then believe that myth as devoutly as any religious person believes in their whacky dogma. We are all, within our own minds, great warriors, misunderstood prophets, unappreciated visionaries, defiant rebels or any number of other archetypal heroes.

Identity is not, I think, a matter of our thoughts and ideas alone. Nor is it simply the culmination of our talents, opinions and idiosyncrasies. Identity is the illusion that our lives have a storyline, that who we are can be found in what we've been through.

My contention is that our lives are meandering and plotless, and though they certainly contain stories, they are not stories in and of themselves. Any semblance of order in our pasts—the notion that every event is linked in some fatalistic way to every preceding and following event—is an illusion manufactured by our needy consciousnesses. We call this illusion self.

I was born. I was raised. I went to school. I quit school. I lazed about for a while. I got a job. I made some money. I lost the money. I started trying to make the money back.

You've just read about my 23 years of life on this planet in one small paragraph. Does it tell a story? Certainly the events are causally related. If I had not been born, I could not have been raised. If I'd not gone to school, I'd have never quit school. If I'd not lost all my money, I'd not be trying to remake it.

Cause and effect are present. Events lead to other events, actions have reactions. There is a beginning. There is (or will be) a middle. There will be an end. So why does my life only have the *illusion* of a storyline?

For the answer, let's look at some men whose lives have been adapted into stories. The movie *Ray,* for instance, tells the life story of Ray Charles, a famous singer and musician. From the movie, we learn that Ray lost his vision as a small child, not long after seeing his brother drown. We see him learning to play music. We see him innovating music. We see him falling in love. We see his marital infidelities. We see his struggles with drug addiction. We see him overcome obstacles and earn his place as one of the most famous musicians of all time.

The movie was a story, for certain, but was Ray Charles' life a story? I'd say no. These moments we see in the film have been embellished, idealized and edited together to make the audience draw conclusions that would not be entirely apparent if we were privy to all the events that occurred in the vast gulf of years between them. Given the same facts about his life, different writers and directors could tell entirely different stories. The movie leads us to draw a conclusion that if Ray's brother hadn't drowned, Ray would never have become the genius that he was. This might be true, but it's not a certainty. Cause and effect are at work in our lives, but often obliquely.

People often say, "If only Hitler had gotten into art school."

What if he had? Who's to say that he wouldn't have still perpetrated the evil that he did? He might have quit art school after a year and then found himself shortly thereafter on the same path that he would have taken had he been rejected.

My friend Cody views himself as a heroic failure who bucked everyone's expectations of him and broke free of the shackles of their ambitions for him. Let's look at the facts from which this archetypal Cody Weber was drawn (We can't really know these to be facts, because they were relayed to us by a biased party, but we will not presume Cody a liar):

1. Cody was expected to do well in life.
2. Cody did not do well in life.

Based upon just these two facts, we can make Cody Weber fit any number of archetypes. We can make him a hero who stood up against the role others were trying to impose on him. We can make him a weakling who buckled under the pressure of those who wanted him to achieve great things. We can make him an ingrate who spurned the love and support of his family out of pure spite. We can make him a spoiled brat who glutted himself on everyone's love and admiration to the point that he took it for granted.

How can we know which of these are true? How can we know if *any* of them are true? Surely there is a cause for what Cody perceives to be his failure—but why is it necessarily to be found in the support of his family? Perhaps it was caused by a chemical imbalance or an event that no one would think to tie to said failure? Further, how do we know—and how does Cody really know, for that matter—that his family really did expect a lot of him or that he really is a failure? In the former case, memory has been shown to be far less reliable than we would comfortably be able to admit[1] and in the later case his failure is contingent upon

---

[1] **Eyewitness Memory Is Unreliable** by Marc Green
http://www.visualexpert.com/Resources/eyewitnessmemory.html

his personal definition of the word. Those who admire his brilliant photography[2] certainly do not view him as a failure.

Under scrutiny, our narratives fall apart. They are our fragile and inadequate attempts to bully our lives into making sense. We haven't the proper tools to make any real sense of things. Our memories are shoddy, our objectivity in matters of self is dubious and the effects we assign to certain causes are likely more often wrong than not.

If my original precept that identity is largely derived from our narrative for ourselves holds true under scrutiny, then in diminishing the veracity of said narrative, I have also dealt a blow to our current concept of identity. I think that this is far too counterintuitive to have any real impact on our perceptions of self, but if it can be accepted as truth, then I think there is a great deal of freedom (and danger) to be found in it.

To say that perception is truth is something of a banal cliché at this point, but to assert that *how we choose* to perceive the events of our lives can actually change our identity entirely would give us the ability to control who we are (at least in our own eyes) to an extent rarely dreamed possible in the age of genetic determinism.

To clarify, I don't believe that these perceptions can turn someone who is by almost all accounts a villain into a hero, only

---

[2] **The Photography of Cody Weber**
http://www.myspace.com/weberphoto

that it can make such a person believe that he or she is heroic. Of course, villains throughout the ages have always fancied themselves heroes—this is nothing new.

Hitler did not see an evil man in the mirror.

The difference in my line of thinking is that it makes such delusions permissible by their ubiquity. In other words, if all men are delusional in regards to their self, then who can say that one man's delusion is any less or more untrue than any other man's delusion? By what means, if my reasoning holds largely cogent, would we be able to dispute a villain's claims of heroicness or a failure's perception of success? If identity is delusion, then all perception is undermined and no ethical barometer can be said to possess any objectivity since the good guys are only good in their heads and the bad guys are probably good in theirs as well.

Some will here make the argument that ethics lay outside the will and that good guys are good regardless of their perception of themselves and that acts of evil are evil regardless of whether or not evil was the intent of the malefactor who perpetrated them. If God is that outside force, that non-human moral barometer, than I would like to see proof not only of him but proof of his will. And if that non-human mechanism of morality is not God then what is it?

Richard Dawkins, the famed evolutionary biologist and an outspoken advocate of atheism and rationalism, outlined in his best-selling work *The God Delusion*, his evolutionary explanation for the origin of morality and ethics. He explains how things like kin selection and game theory have imbued man with a natural sense of right and wrong. While I don't disagree with his assertions I have to ask why a moral code that evolved is one that need be followed? We evolved instincts towards violence and, if the God gene[3] hypothesis is correct, belief itself—and yet no thinking person views non-violence or non-belief as impossible (and only a strange few thinking people find them immoral). An evolved or *natural* morality is a morality that can be challenged on an intellectual basis in the same way that the value of an evolved predilection towards violence or endocannibalism or rape as a means of reproduction can be challenged. Any evolved social trait can be challenged. No evolutionary biologist that I have ever heard of has made or provided evidence for the assertion that evolution is infallible or has our happiness at heart.

So, if Hitler views himself a good man and no concrete ethical code exists to contradict his goodness, then can we say that our mass perception of him as a villain overrides 1930's Germany's perception of him as a hero? Or his perception of himself as such?

Returning to Cody, does it matter how much his admirers view him as a genius when he views his own work as ugly and wholly lacking in beauty (as he once confessed to me)? I think that it doesn't. I think that a billion voices telling a man who believes he is Thing A that he is actually Thing B are useless if that man's

---

[3] **The God Gene: How Faith Is Hardwired Into Our Genes** by Dean H Hamer
http://www.amazon.com/God-Gene-Faith-Hardwired-Genes/dp/0385500580

perception of himself is unshakable.

If a genocidal maniac is called evil, he can always escape into a more comfortable identity. *I'm not evil*, he might tell himself, *I'm misunderstood. I'm heroically doing what I know is right, even though the odds are against me. I'm reluctantly doing what is necessary to create a better future. I am a visionary.*

Our disgust with such people and what we perceive as their shoddy justifications for their evil actions is nearly universal. Few human beings on this planet today are not aghast at genocide and contemptuous of genocidal maniacs. We so deeply feel this repulsion towards mass violence that any belief system that doesn't hold such people as objectively vile seems unpalatable to many of us, myself included.

I just can't see a way around it, however. I'll restate my logic from start to finish in the briefest terms possible and hopefully someone can provide me the solace of showing me where I am mistaken.

1. Identity is based largely on the illusion of a narrative and the establishment of an archetype of self within that narrative.
2. This narrative is erroneous in every single human being.
3. It is impossible to object to a delusional perception of self in another human being when one's own perception of one's own self is demonstrably delusional as well. To do so

would be an act of hypocrisy and inconsistent with the hitherto defined parameters of human discourse. In other words, the pot cannot call the kettle black (the kettle remains black, but the pot's blackness negates this criticism or makes it universal and thus pragmatically irrelevant).

4. Because delusion is invariable and presumably inescapable, no one sense of self can be seen as superior in veracity to another.
5. An evil man who perceives himself as good cannot be contradicted by other men (for reasons explained in supposition #3) or by an established system of ethics because ethics is either derived from

a. **man**, who is delusional and cannot rightly judge other men's deluded narratives.
b. **God,** who cannot be verified to exist. Even if we simply made the huge assumption of his existence, his will regarding our behavior (if he even has one) would not be readily known to us.
c. **Nature,** which can be disputed, as shown by all manner of precedent.

It's hardly original to argue against a concrete good and evil, but surely in the face of genocide and mass murder, we would be better served if such an objective morality (or ethical truth if you prefer) was somehow in place.

We find ourselves in an unenviable position. We can choose to persist in the deluded view of moral certitudes and objective right and wrong or we can accept that no such thing exists and attempt to justify our persecution of evil in other ways.

Honor: Another String Tied To The Human Marionette, Nothing More.

A friend of mine said of me recently, "I'm friends with TJ for the same reason people keep snakes as pets—the snake is fun and cool and really interesting to watch, but of course you don't expect to get any warmth or compassion from it." He went on to say that I possess an "utter lack of humanity."

Should such a thing bother me? I must admit that I have long been aware that I lack certain sentiments that seem to widely characterize my species, but I've never thought of myself as lacking humanity. I seceded from it, sure. But that's just a cute thing to say to make everyone say, "Wow, that guy sure is hardcore!" and cream their jeans in unrestrained admiration for my greatness.

I must confess though, I do find many human conventions quite antiquated and wholly unworthy of the attention of 21st century people. Honor, for instance, that long revered staple of masculinity and masculine values, holds no weight at all with me. I find myself bizarrely perplexed when others expect me to be beholden to it.

A recent example involves a bet that I made with a YouTube user going by the moniker of BigEvasive. BigEvasive was looking very forward to this year's summer blockbuster *The Incredible Hulk*, which was a franchise reboot of director Ang Lee's 2003 flop *Hulk*. I told him that, in my opinion, The Hulk was a stupid character and it didn't really matter who directed or acted in a film about him, because the source material is simply not of sufficient quality to inspire anything but a mediocre film.

This argument eventually turned into a bet that *The Incredible Hulk* would far surpass "Hulk" in critical accolades. For our wager we used the critical consensus site Rotten Tomatoes[4], which compiles hundreds of film reviews, categorizes them into two classes—fresh and rotten—then averages them out in order to come up with a rough over-all picture of what critics thought of any given film. "Hulk" had received a freshness rating of 61%, which meant that 61% of the reviews that Rotten Tomatoes had compiled had given the film a positive review. In order for BigEvasive to win the bet, "The Incredible Hulk" had to surpass the original by a statistically significant margin. We determined the margin to be 5 percentage points. In other words, it had to receive a freshness rating of 66% or higher in order for him to win the bet.

The stakes were that if he lost, I had to paint myself green and make a video where I behaved like The Incredible Hulk. If he lost, he had to dress as Marilyn Monroe and sing *Happy Birthday To You* to me.

"The Incredible Hulk" opened and reached a freshness rating of 68%[5].

I had lost the bet. Now it was time to pay up. Or was it? BigEvasive was located all the way in Canada and I knew him well

---

[4] http://www.rottentomatoes.com/
[5] It should be noted that "Top Critics" (meaning critics actually employed with reputable publications), gave the movie only 59%.

enough to know he was too chickenshit to really put me in any sort of difficult position if I neglected to fulfill my end of the bargain. Honor never factored into my decision to "welch" on our bet. I didn't feel that warm and tingly masculine ethic tugging at my heartstrings, informing my conscience that I would be diminished in some profound way if I didn't paint myself green and gallivant around smashing things in the fashion of a third-rate comic book character.

As ridiculous and sophomoric as the whole situation was, the small backlash that it inspired[6] set my mind to wondering as to the exact nature of honor. It's a word that we all hear tossed around a lot, but I for one have never had the concept explained to me.

Consulting the dictionary was useless. It contained 13 separate definitions of the word, all of which fell staggeringly short of encapsulating the word as it is most commonly used. It became obvious that if I wanted a definition to the word honor, I'd have to figure it out myself.

I started by Googling the word by itself and seeing what came up. Wikipedia's entry was meaningless, other than some interesting etymological notes.

What caught my eye were pages pertaining to the Medal of Honor, which is the absolute highest decoration offered by the US

---

[6] Halfwits of all shapes and sizes informed me that I was an honorless mongrel and that they thought far less of me than they had previously. Why they imagined I would care what anonymous slanderers on the internet thought of me as a person, I cannot say.

military. It is given to a soldier if he (or she, I suppose) distinguished himself *"...conspicuously by gallantry and intrepidity at the risk of his life above and beyond the call of duty while engaged in an action against an enemy of the United States."*

Let's dissect that, shall we?

In other words, the military defines honor as risking your life to kill people in service to them. Not just risking your life though—because all soldiers do that. You have to pretty much walk into certain death (when it's not even necessary or expected of you) to get awarded a Medal of Honor.

As I went further and further down the list I discovered samurai codes of honor, honor killings and other specific examples of honor—but mostly I waded through the endless litany of fluff surrounding the word. After about an hour of research and a number of days spent in contemplation, I drew this conclusion: honor is nothing more than strict adherence to a completely arbitrary code of conduct.

The more strictly you follow the code, the more honor you have. The more staunchly you interpret the code, the more honor you have. Honor and obedience are remarkably interchangeable concepts. Allow me to demonstrate:

She has dishonored our faith by not entering into an arranged marriage.

Sheila has disobeyed our faith by not entering into an arranged marriage.

Lieutenant Gilroy behaved dishonorably when he gave our position to the enemy.

Lieutenant Gilroy behaved disobediently when he gave our position to the enemy.

The fact that I would not paint myself green to fulfill my end of a bet shows that I have no honor.

The fact that I would not paint myself green to fulfill my end of a bet shows that I have no obedience (to the system of betting and bet fulfillment).

Once one comes to the understanding that honor is nothing more than adherence to a particular code of conduct, one is less inclined to lament its absence in one's self. I have never fancied myself an obedient person and I have little in the way of tolerance for those who do. I adhere to no code of honor because to do so would be to dishonor myself.

    Many will make the argument that strict adherence to certain social codes are a necessity to facilitate a stable society. These people are the unwisest of souls—those who have not yet realized that we must be bound together by our common ideas, not *made common* by the act of binding ourselves to the ideas imposed upon us by a given overlord. In other words, we must unite around our goals, not expect our goals to unite us.

The concept of honor, as I have adequately defined it, is inarguably a detriment to the end goal of getting humans to acknowledge existent harmony rather than strive for artificial harmony through the coerced recognition of codes of conduct that expand well beyond what any given individual would acknowledge as necessary. Honor has long been a tool to keep those who benefit from obedience (namely, those who are obeyed) in control.

We are essentially beings who, in our boundless capacity for delusion, stitch random events, emotions and sensations together into a tapestry called "identity." We reinforce our narrative by comparing it to the equally flawed narratives of our fellow human beings. Those who reinforce our narratives are friends. Those who contradict our narratives are enemies. Thus, the currency of other people's opinions is vital to our sense of cohesion. This is why loners are often incomprehensible; It's because without the steady influence and reinforcement of the tribe, their narratives topple in on themselves or becomes muddled and idiosyncratic. Those in power—CEO's, Senators, Celebrities, Journalists—are all what I'd like to term "super-reinforcers." Super-reinforcers are those who have enough influence to propagate a particular narrative over a larger sphere of human beings than typical reinforcers.

For example, your friend who agrees with you that your girlfriend is a skank because she cheated on you is a reinforcer, because he is supporting your narrative. If you watch a TV show where a girl who cheats on her boyfriend under similar circumstances as those in your life then everyone involved in that TV show is a super-reinforcer because they not only reinforced your notion that your girlfriend is a skank, but they're likely reinforcing the narratives of thousands of people who are or have been or will be in your situation. It is natural to feel affection towards those who reinforce your ideas about yourself.

Your girlfriend meanwhile, seeks out her friends to assure her that she is not a skank, but that she acted out because you neglected her. Her friends will support this idea and there are plenty of TV shows, movies, books and role-model super-reinforcers to back up her narrative as well.

Unfortunately because your narrative casts her as a slut who can't say no to any offer of cock and her narrative casts you as a cold and distant shell of a man who is incapable of love, you will not reinforce each other's narratives. It is this, more than the pain of any indiscretion, that will drive you apart.

This is why honor is such an effective control mechanism. It promises to turn all perception against you if you behave disobediently. It says to you—if you deviate from our idea of good, then you will be devoid of reinforcers.

Honor uses reverence as a currency—those who adhere to the given code are given ample amounts of reverence. Those who do not adhere are given none of the currency of reverence. They are, in fact, denigrated and despised by the people. This sometimes culminates in a sickening ritual, practiced mostly by Muslims, called honor killings.

Honor killings are when a female[7] is murdered by her family for dishonoring the code of their religion[8]. According to a leading website on honor killings[9] "Over 5,000 women and girls are killed every year by family members in so-called 'honor killings', according to the UN. These crimes occur where cultures believe that a woman's unsanctioned sexual behavior brings such shame on the family that any female accused or suspected must be murdered. Reasons for these murders can be as trivial as talking to a man, or as innocent as suffering rape"[10]

What man, other than a violent sociopathic, would murder his own daughter because she was raped? A religious one.

Religions have codes, and if one doesn't adhere to those codes, one will seem dishonorable. And apparently, for 5,000 families each year, the loss of daughter seems a small price to pay to avoid the loss of honor.

So, when a politician or a commentator gets on the airwaves and starts weeping and wailing that honor is a dead

---

[7] There are a decent number of instanced of males being killed in honor killings, but it's not nearly so widespread.
[8] I say religion, rather than society or culture (which is what the political correctness police would have me say), because honor killings seem to transcend culture. Even here in the US, honor killings seem to have started taking place. http://news.yahoo.com/s/huffpost/20080709/cm_huffpost/111549
[9] http://www.stophonourkillings.com/
[10] Spellings have been Americanized.

concept here in America, my response is, "good." When the reverence of others is more important to people than their own loved ones, something sick is happening.

Honor has the right to exist only as a guideline, pinning you to your own ethical standards. When you replace your own will and desire with another man's will or desire solely to maintain honor in the eyes of others, you have become a puppet. You've allowed your own dissent to be weaponized against you and you have undermined your individuality.

Where's the honor in that?

Instant Gratification

This section is dedicated to Scotty and Evelyn, respectively the smartest and cutest accidents I know.

It's my belief that people are basically selfish to the point of self-defeat, that in their attempts to secure their personal happiness they destroy everything that could ever bring them happiness.

We're always willing to make the worst bargain in the world: a little bit of here-and-now-joy for a heaping helping of down-and-out-misery down the road. As a species we pollute our planet because cars and factories are spiffy conveniences; we don't give a tall glass of fuck that our children might grow up in a world made of shit and smoke.

As individuals we have unprotected sex, resulting in diseases to wipe us out and in kids we can't afford (because we spend all our money on worthless impulse buys that consistently fail to live up to their promises of making our lives complete). We do this for nothing more than a single moment of bliss—an orgasm lasting no longer than a few seconds. From that pursuit of tiny happiness comes massive misery!

We drink now, saying "fuck you!" to our future livers. We smoke now, saying "eat shit!" to our future lungs.

This is not an original observation by any stretch of even the imagination. Pundits and other assorted fuckwits have yammered on about our culture of "instant gratification" for as long as I can remember. So why am I bothering to harp on this old and established bit of cynicism?

Because I aim to defend it.

Intellectuals may oft lament the limited long-term planning abilities of their fellow human beings, but rarely have I heard folks extol the many virtues of our widespread inability to prioritize on a large timescale. Not once have I heard a man or woman give thanks to our tendency to make the devil's deal of short term pleasure at the cost of long-term contentment. The benefits of our instant gratification tendency, hereafter referred to as IGT, are largely unsung.

The first and most obvious thing that IGT provides for us are children. In 2001, 49% of all pregnancies in America were unintended[11]. As a man who hates babies and usually cares even less for the adults that they grow into, I must still begrudgingly admit that it's a good thing that they exist. The continuation of the human race is, even in the eyes of a misanthropist like me, a good thing. If we assume that those 49% of Americans in 2001 hadn't had their babies because they were smart people who were able to plan ahead and realize they couldn't afford kids, then half of the 7-year-olds annoying the piss out of you today wouldn't be alive. That sounds good on the surface, but consider this: if half the people alive didn't exist, there are only half as many chances of some asshole hitting the genetic lottery and becoming the next Richard Dawkins, Salvador Dali or Steven Spielberg.

Now before you make the argument that those 49% of

---

[11] http://www.guttmacher.org/pubs/psrh/full/3809006.pdf

babies that were unplanned are the offspring of people too dumb to take even the slightest precautions against pregnancy (and, we can extrapolate, STDs) and are therefore almost certainly idiots themselves whose children are likely to be as dumb as their parents, I'd remind you of three important facts.

1. It is perfectly possible for intelligent people to fall victim to the powerful force of IGT, especially in the area of sex, where powerful chemical impulses can overcome our better judgment like a hurricane can overcome flimsy lawn furniture. We can prove this by looking at the number of exceptional geniuses throughout history who have contracted sexually transmitted diseases. Even in recent times, where condoms are readily available to all, a number of famous authors, playwrights, film and literary critics contracted the AIDS virus[12].

2. It is perfectly possible for two unintelligent people to produce intelligent offspring. Neither my mother nor my father had blue eyes, but both my brother and I do. The reason for this is because we both received a recessive gene from each parent to "give" us blue eyes.

---

[12] **http://en.wikipedia.org/wiki/List_of_HIV-positive_people**
One could make the argument that because these men (and a few women) mostly contracted the disease before it was well known that their lack of caution was somewhat understandable. I counter by pointing out that there were still a large number of known STDs at the time that most of these (typically gay) men contracted the disease, so my point that sexual urges can overcome the good sense of even learned and intelligent people still holds water.

Intelligence is a lot more complex a trait then eye color, but the principle is the same. Genes that are dormant in two stupid people could become active in the offspring of said people and result in a child smarter than the dumb asses that spawned it.

3. Stupid people serve a number of vital functions in our society. They cook our burgers, lay our brick and keep comedians like Adam Sandler and Larry The Cable Guy successful. No one with an IQ west of 110 is going to want to work the register at *Taco Bell*, yet plenty of MENSA members are still going to need Double-Decker Taco Supremes and Cinnamon Twists—so let's all agree that idiots in this country, though unpleasant company, pull their weight.

IGT keeps us cranking out kids, ensuring that we have a stable population even in this age of easy contraception. If the overpopulation fears of alarmist liberals are anything to worry about, then I'll point out that IGT also keeps us dying at a healthy rate from preventable things like STDs, heart-disease and lung cancer. IGT may well be the sole stabilizing force of our population! It keeps us breeding and it keeps us dying.

Another advantage of IGT keeping us from living too long is that far less of us survive into senility than medical science, combined with reasonable health awareness, ought to rightfully allow us to do. This spares us from the worst years of our lives.

Just recently my great grandma, who has survived to the

miserable old age of 96, told my gay[13] uncle that she doubted that my aunt's daughter was really my aunt's. Why? Because my aunt is such a slut that she probably cheated on her husband. In my grandma's senile and faltering old brain that doesn't just call the paternity of my cousin into question, but her maternity as well! I hate to spout a tough guy cliché, but if I'm ever that old and stupid, please shoot me.

Thankfully, my proclivity for donuts and cheese and processed meats to the disregard of my health will likely send me to an early grave like my father before me. Thanks to IGT, I will likely die with my wits intact and my family will be able to remember me as a mean-spirited old fucker who hated everyone and was damned hilarious.

You may be saying at this point, "Okay, perhaps there is something of an argument to be made for benefits of personal IGT, but on a societal level, it's all bad news!" I will grant you that IGT creates problems like global warming and peak oil, but if not for our reckless use of oil and petroleum based products, we'd likely not be as far along in our research of alternative energy because our frugality in the face of a crisis would have had us managing our oil better and using it longer. If it weren't for the global warming problem we'd not have poured nearly as much many into climate science, which has lead us to a number of auxiliary revelations about how our whole ecosystem works. Scientific

---

[13] His sexuality isn't really pertinent here, but it's how I personally identify him. If I just said "my uncle," that would be sufficient for you, but it would not ring right to my ears.

discovery and innovation have always been driven by crises. Aviation technology has been pushed forward more by war and the need to stay ahead of enemy competition than it has out of love of science. Microwaves, Velcro, thermal imagining, prosthetic limb advancements and even the computer networking techniques that eventually led to the creation of the internet were all designed or perfected by the military for the purpose of being more effective as a killing machine.

    IGT is a force that creates problems that only science can fix—it is my contention that the two things are symbiotic and that if we were a species less prone to getting into mischief, we would lack a great deal of the scientific and technological sophistication that we possess today.

Obey Your Master

"Creating a life that reflects your values and satisfies your soul is a rare achievement. In a culture that relentlessly promotes avarice and excess as the good life, a person happy doing his own work is usually considered an eccentric, if not a subversive. Ambition is only understood if it's to rise to the top of some imaginary ladder of success. Someone who takes an undemanding job because it affords him the time to pursue other interests and activities is considered a flake. A person who abandons a career in order to stay home and raise children is considered not to be living up to his potential-as if a job title and salary are the sole measure of human worth. You'll be told in a hundred ways, some subtle and some not, to keep climbing, and never be satisfied with where you are, who you are, and what you're doing. There are a million ways to sell yourself out, and I guarantee you'll hear about them."

Those are the words of Bill Watterson, the creator of the comic strip Calvin & Hobbes which ran from 1985 to 1995. Bill Watterson is a strange breed of person. People, on a subconscious level, feel that his mentality is a threat to the American dream. The American dream being, of course, making fat sums of money. When Steven Spielberg called Bill because he was interested in making a Calvin & Hobbes movie, Bill just turned him down flat. That's incredible. In this culture, shunning greed is the utmost sin, the most unforgivable and incomprehensible outrage. When he refused to license his characters (all those truck decals you see with Calvin peeing on rival truck brands were made without licensing) to make a profit, he was essentially making the statement that the integrity of his artistic creation was more valuable than any sum of money, than any life of comfort.

As much as I adore and admire his resolve, I do not perceive that sort of integrity in myself and allusions to such integrity would be illusions. However, just because I lack Mr. Watterson's immense and incorruptible virtue does not mean that I lack all virtue or that I cannot recognize the validity of his virtuousness or admire the strength of his convictions, just as I have gotten a great many people to admire the strength of my various convictions by becoming a public-speaker, sometimes-comedian and freedom-advocate on the popular internet website YouTube[14].

Honor has essentially exploited our tendency to admire those of great resolve by standardizing morality. Our admiration is permissible, in the eyes of the powerful, only when it is directed towards their ideal. Their ideal, it should be noted, is never the ideal that they themselves live by. It's the ideal that most conveniences them to have others live by.

Let me say here that I don't for a moment believe in the idea of CEO's and Politicians as arch-villains dividing and conquering the populace with ingenious deceptions and carefully-crafted propaganda. I think this vile tendency emerged quite naturally over the course of our social evolution and have

---

[14] My account can be located here: *http://youtube.com/user/TheAmazingAtheist*

rarely, if ever, been conscious acts of malevolence.

And because this tendency has been hardwired into us by evolution, it can only be overcome with cognition. There is a good reason why so few films financed by major studios encourage introspection—it is subconsciously perceived as detrimental to the agenda of the corporations, which is to keep the population dull and complacent. Only people disconnected enough from any sense of self to watch MTV would be undiscerning enough to inhale the glut of insipid and intoxicating miasma known to mankind simply as "commercials."

Honor is used to teach us who to admire and who to revile. Those who adhere to the social codes for their given class—99% of celebrities and athletes—are admired and revered because of the misdirection of our natural love of those with strong convictions towards those who have only the strong convictions approved by those in power.

Those in power despise with infinite vitriol the Bill Watterson's of the world because the ethic that he exhibits is not conducive to their vision of utopia, wherein everything and everyone is for sale; where art is nothing more than a product to be cynically peddled to the masses for a little capital gain.

What upsets the powerful more than anything about Watterson's case is that to berate him openly would have displayed to the whole world what they really were. Despite all of our programming to the contrary, many human beings can still recognize genuine integrity when they see it—which is why occasionally the powerful let someone with genuine integrity infiltrate the mainstream. Usually they do it on accident and, when they've realized their mistake, cannot possible fix the problem as long as the individual of integrity is successful. To do so would be to declare themselves open enemies of true integrity and undermine their unquestioned authority.

I fear, however, that the day is fast approaching when few people will recognize true integrity and the powerful will be in the position to oppose it openly. It's as Bill said. *"A person happy doing his own work is usually considered an eccentric, if not a subversive."*

What merely seems eccentric today may be called subversive tomorrow. And what is merely subversive today may become unforgivable tomorrow.

The "pursuit of happiness" that our founders [15] felt important enough to call an inalienable right in The Declaration of Independence is now viewed as evil by the majority of Americans. Of course, if you sat most of Americans down and said, "Do you believe in the pursuit of happiness?" they'd nod their empty heads until the sound of the spare change rattling around in their skulls gave you a migraine—yet, those who truly pursue happiness are cast in a villainous light. The enterprising young businessman in the slums who tries to make money selling drugs that the US government doesn't approve of will find himself crushed beneath

---

[15] Apologies to non-American readers.

police truncheons because, as Chris Rock so astutely pointed out, "Only the white man is allowed to profit from other people's pain." I would substitute the word "normal" instead of the "white" but otherwise have no qualms with his statement.

The pursuit of happiness cannot only be for the rich, the well-connected or those willing to sell their souls for table scraps from the big corporate banquet. If happiness is to truly be an inalienable right than laws must only be passed and enforced when the cost of one man's happiness is the destruction of another man's will. The drug dealer peddles his wares to drug users who have a choice—they can choose to take drugs or not to take drugs. The murderer's victims have no choice—which is why murder must remain illegal. The murderer's right to the pursuit of happiness must be alienable to safeguard to inalienable rights of others.

This does not, however, make the urges of a murderer evil—they're simply not pragmatic. If the murder finds a willing victim, one who wishes to by killed because he is tired of life (or for some other reason), then said murderer can pursue his happiness without violating the right to another's happiness.

We are here making the assumption that our lives are the property of our selves—which is the assumption that our founders, despite their slave-owning hypocrisy, made when they founded this country of rugged individualists who reviled the authority of the crown of England.

This idea is contrary to all presently popular socio-theological-political models. We are viewed by a great many as property of a God whose will is known to us only through the 5,000- to 2,000-year-old desert scribblings of Jewish nomads. Our lives are seen by those who subscribe to this ludicrous fairytale as nothing more than kindling to stoke the fires of Hell or drones whose sole purpose is to act out the will of their fictional deity.

Others see us as belonging to the state. The state can decide what's best for us, take our money to create weapons for our soldiers to use to attack countries that we have nothing against. And if too many of our soldiers die, they've no qualms about ordering citizens to fight in their wars. "Fight or go to prison" is the choice they give us, all while claiming that we're fighting for "freedom." What freedom? Their freedom to tell you what to do? Their freedom to conscript you into an army and make you kill your fellow man for the sake of a cause that you'll never understand? Their freedom to send you to your death the moment that your death will fatten their pockets in the slightest?

You are not free as long as you are the property of a God or a government. You are only free when you are the master of your fate and the captain of your soul. The elections that they hold are nothing more than a means of placating you with fake freedom, whilst strategically keeping you from the historical understanding of what true freedom entails. It is as Benjamin Franklin once said: "Democracy is three wolves and a sheep voting on dinner. Liberty is a well armed sheep contesting the result."

When you allow yourself to be fodder for the wars of powerful men, you are not well-armed sheep contesting the result. You are pawns on a chessboard, viewed by the King and Queen as wholly expendable from a larger strategic perspective.

If you kill enough for them and are brave and selfless (what a terrible thing to be) enough for them, you could win a Medal of Honor. You could be a hero, like Ira Hayes who raised the flag at Iwo Jima in that famous picture and died drunk face down in a ditch lying in his own vomit and blood a number of years later.

The currency of honor does not buy a means to the pursuit of happiness. Rather, it further indebts you to your owners—the CEO, the senator, the judges and cops and prison guards. And they've shown—from their inability to take care of the heroes at Iwo Jima or the heroes of 9/11[16]—that no matter how much you give them, they won't give anything back.

The people are told to be selfless while the politicians, justice system officials and corporate cocksuckers are free to be selfish. You're told to not pursue your happiness, while they whip

---

[16] http://www.firerescue1.com/news/233790/
Excerpt: *"About 40,000 people — law-enforcement officers, firefighters, transit workers and others, many of whom were volunteers — converged on southern Manhattan five years ago to help in the rescue and recovery efforts after the attack on the World Trade Center. A study by Mount Sinai Medical Center shows 70 percent of those workers have respiratory problems."*

The government has refused to pay for healthcare for these men and women, many of whom were volunteers. You give to America and America gives nothing back other than vague allusions to the concept of freedom that mean nothing upon even the most rudimentary examination.

your backs bloody and sustain themselves on your blood like the vampiric assholes they are.

And if you complain about your lot in life and demand your fair share of the pie, they start whining about their rights. They talk about the fruits of *their* labor, while you're the one working in the factory and they're the ones shuffling papers in an air-conditioned office making huge salaries. They call you a socialist, as if the word itself were an instant argument winner because they've imagined and sold you a consensus that says "socialism is bad" and socialism means whatever they want it to mean. They know that you don't know what it means and use your ignorance to control you.

"Honor" Thyself

Without reinforcers of any kind, our idiosyncrasies compound to the point that we are no longer able to function in normal society. We are social animals who need the approval of our fellow beings to maintain a coherent sense of self.

Conversely, if we play by the rules and allow ourselves to be influenced by others, we find ourselves to victims of the nightmares of the pecking order.

In 1921 a Norwegian zoologist named Thorleif Schjelderup-Ebbe (don't worry, I can't pronounce it either) discovered a strange behavior exhibited by chickens during their feeding time. The weaker birds would refuse to eat until the stronger birds had their fill. He called this occurrence the pecking order and it occurs in all animals in one form or another—the perceived weak willfully succumb to the perceived strong.

In nature, the behavior that lends itself most to social advancement is aggressiveness. The willingness to relentlessly attack all those who oppose you makes you dangerous and will, even in our supposedly enlightened species, bring you to power. Have you ever wondered why loan sharks kill those who cannot pay them? Surely a living man is always more likely to repay a loan than a dead one! It's not a necessity of their business, but it is a necessity of their perceived dominance within the territories under their control.

Criminals conduct themselves in this fashion because they have not yet socially evolved to the point where they've recognized the power of reinforcer-denial as an even more potent control mechanism than old-school brutality. Many government (and aspiring governments) in countries that we (in all of our American arrogance) label "underdeveloped" or "the third world" still enforce their dictates with the sloppy and outmoded use of physical violence.

We are not the least bit better than any of these countries in most respects. Our sole advantage is that we have devised[17] a more cunning thing to take away from people than their lives. We take away their ability to regulate their self-image through the social and cultural reinforcement of their personal narratives. We steal their identities.

The only possible means of countervailing this identity-theft [18] is to recognize the manipulation as it happens and consciously defy its influence. This can be achieved in several ways, but before we can even begin to discuss them, you have to figure out who what narrative you would truly prefer.

Because your identity is inexorably tied to those around you, pay attention to who you gravitate towards, who you idolize, who you admire. Then ask yourself if you really admire what they're selling, or if you merely fear not buying it. Never allow yourself to be motivated by fear. Fear can be levied against you to make you behave in ways that you otherwise would not. The first step towards self-realization is the renunciation of fear.

---

[17] I use this word lightly here. It wasn't truly a conscious decision on our part.
[18] I know the term's already taken, but fuck it.

Ah, but some fear does you a service. The fear of prison likely keeps you out of prison. The fear of snakes will prevent snake bites. The fear of losing your life will prevent you from risking it foolishly.

So embrace those fears if you choose. The type of fear you must renounce is a far more subtle and devious variety of fear. It is fear of inadequacy, fear of being judged, fear of the wrath of the super-reinforcers.

Luckily, this fear can be destroyed by the very solution to the identity-theft problem. It was simply important that you acknowledged your fears before attempting these methods.

Lone Wolf. Is it possible to maintain one's cohesion even without reinforcement? With constant strength of will, I believe that some people can do so. However, a life without any interaction whatsoever is bound to be savagely lonely. Even the most virulent misanthrope would likely be heavily taxed by such an isolated existence Combine that with the sheer exertion of maintaining your psyche in a vacuum and you're a train wreck waiting to happen.

Subversive. The simple act of awareness is enough to largely free you from the bondage of societal synchronicity. When you are aware of the constant manipulation of all those around you, you're less likely to be impacted by it. The drawback here is that you live a life of utter paranoia, always wondering if you really like what you like and really hate what you hate.

Counter-Culture. Don't like the values of the *vox populi?* Create your own value system and find others with similar ones. Once this was hard, but in the internet age it's significantly simpler. The drawback is that such groups can become too clickish and cult-like.

Ultimately, no solution is the perfect solution. They all have their share of pros and cons—but even at their most problematic they are preferable to the bland life of servitude that I thoroughly criticized in the previous section.

My Various Failed Subversive Revolutions

This chapter is something of an aside that explains my credentials as a revolutionary. They are less than impressive and often make me appear entirely repugnant, but I trust they will be amusing to many of you.

The ASU

Atheist Scum United was founded on April 4th, 2007[19] with the purpose of pissing a lot of people off. It quickly came under fire from moderate atheists for its extremist stances and hostile conduct, and imploded on May 5th 2007[20], just barely a month after it had launched.

The tactics, which included spam attacks on Christian websites, driving Christians off of public forums like YouTube and forming a lobby to get children removed from fundamentalist households, were loathed by all but the most authoritarian secularists.

Its true purpose was to elevate me to cult-leader status and build a following of extremist adulators to funnel money into my pocket and obey my directives, which would have always been aimed at wreaking social havoc.

Sadly, because of my home environment at the time and the stupidity of those who I exploited as partners in the venture,

---

[19] http://www.youtube.com/watch?v=2wdo98GAvmA
[20] http://www.youtube.com/watch?v=9BlXCMv78Uk

the whole thing went to hell in a hand basket. Private documents explaining ASU tactics leaked to the public before they had been polished down into something more bland and inoffensive and the backlash was tremendous. The ASU wound up spending all of its time defending its own existence and soon collapsed under the weight of its own bloated incompetence. It remains my most public attempt at destroying the social order and my most public failure.

Feminist Rape Plot

In 2005 and 2006 I posed as an extremist feminist named Martha Stanton[21] who advocated a number of extreme measures for creating a matriarchal society on various online forums and in a few small newsletters. Of the numerous opinions of Martha Stanton, I shall illuminate a few:

7. The rape of men through the use of alcohol (or other intoxicating agents) and large strap-on dildos. The stated objective here was to make men realize that they could be victims as well, thus engendering new empathy between the sexes.

8. Many feminist extremists (hereafter referred to as feminazis) advocate the abortion of all male babies, but that wasn't subversive enough for Martha. She instead advocated giving birth to male children but raising them to obey and worship women, to treat them like dogs and to

---

[21] This is not the actual name I used, but for legal purposes, it will suffice here.

never love them.

9. Martha demanded that the word man be stricken from the dictionary and that all words describing manliness of masculinity (such as manliness and masculinity) be removed from the language as well. In doing so, Martha believed that men would lack the ability to express themselves as different from women and the divisions between the sexes would diminish.
10. Martha said that newly-wed brides should have lesbian orgies on the night of their honeymoon and that they should divorce their husbands the next day without ever sleeping with them. I don't even remember her rationale for this one.
11. Martha wanted certain boys to be raised on farms and cultivated as meat for women so that man recognized his place as an animal.
12. Martha wanted 95% of boys castrated at puberty.
13. Martha demanded that only girls be allowed access to education because the violent tendencies of men led them to use their education only to make bombs and guns.

Martha's ideas never caught on. She spent most of her time arguing with less extreme feminists (such as all of them) and was banned from countless forums. The newsletters that printed her work subsequently came under fire and would not publish future articles. She did, interestingly enough, acquire a somewhat sizable circle of male sexual submissives in the BDSM lifestyle, but these were useless to her purpose of creating a matriarchy and even more useless to my purpose of fucking the world up royally.

The Pricks & The SSS

As a young lad, I attended the private school of Crestdale[22]. I remember very little about the school, as I am largely a forward-thinking person, not often given to reminiscence. I do, however, recall the school song, taught to us by a balding and hopefully now dead asshole named Dave[23].

> *Crestdale school is number one!*
> *We make learning fu-un!*
> *Well I know!*
> *(clap clap)*
> *Well I know!*
> *(clap clap)*
> *'Cause Crestdale's where I go!*

Even as a boy I found that song to be completely inane drivel. I was fond of some of the other songs we sang, such as *"Ghost of John"* and *"Oh, You Can't Get To Heaven,"* but I digress.

What I remember most of all though were my friends Luke, Nick and What's-His-Face and our two clubs: The SSS (School

---
[22] Once again, for legal reasons, I am not using the real name here.
[23] His name may really have been Dave, actually. I don't quite know.

Sucks Shit) and The Pricks (this name was a double entendre in that we were admittedly asshole and that we all carried around thumbtacks with which to stab other children). I don't recall if School Sucks Shit ever had a theme song, but I know that The Pricks did.

We are the pricks!
We prick you in the dick!
Dow dow dow!
Dow dow dow dow dow!
Dow dow dow!
Dow dow dow dow dow!

Granted, it was only slightly less inane that the Crestdale theme song, but it was a hell of a lot more "*fu-un*".

In either incarnation of our club, our primary agenda was to fuck up our uptight private school, which we all despised with every fiber of our angst-crammed preteen minds. Threatening letters to teachers, harassment, the infliction of tiny puncture wounds upon our peers, lifting up the girl's skirts, making fun of the kid whose older brother had committed suicide—nothing was above or beneath us.

Pretty much all of us were expelled from Crestdale or asked to leave, so I guess we must have been a threat to the established order. At 8-years-old I had managed my first and thusfar my last successful subversive movement.

Democracy Is Fascism By Consensus

I am an atheist in a country with a religious majority, where the majority rules. If ever a law were to come before the voters that somehow restricted the rights of those who do not believe in God, how would they vote? I imagine they would vote similarly to how 11 states voted on the issue of gay marriage in 2004.

The question posed to the American people was simple: do these people deserve the right to enter into the same social contracts that we do? Let's take a look how that turned out.

BAN SAME-SEX MARRIAGE?		
	YES	NO
Arkansas	75%	25%
Georgia	76%	24%
Kentucky	75%	25%
Michigan	59%	41%
Mississippi	86%	14%
Montana	67%	33%
North Dakota	73%	27%
Ohio	62%	24%
Oklahoma	76%	24%
Oregon	57%	43%
Utah	66%	34%

There you have it, Mr. Franklin, three wolves and a sheep voting on what to have for dinner.

Where are the well-armed sheep to contest this vote? Where are those who defy the masses of dumb asses and shove the narrow-minded pettiness of the populace down its own throat? As George Carlin once said, "We don't have people like that in this country."

People must have control over their destiny and the direction of their country, but just as murders cannot murder without consent, populations cannot strip one-another of inalienable rights. If your pursuit of happiness includes fucking other members of your own sex, then it is un-American for us to put it to a vote. If desegregation were put to a vote, blacks might still be drinking from the black water fountain and we certainly wouldn't have a man named Barack Hussein Obama in the highest office in the land.

A system where 51% of the people can rule over the other 49% doesn't make much sense, either ethically or pragmatically. Having a leader who only represents the values of a little over half of your country makes no sense. The fictional character spider Jerusalem from Warren Ellis' comic book masterpiece *Transmetropolitan* explained it best:

"You want to know about voting? I'm here to tell you about voting. Imagine you're locked in a huge underground nightclub filled with sinners, whores, freaks and unnamable things that rape pit bulls for fun. And you ain't allowed out until you all vote on what you're going to do tonight. **You** *like to put your feet up and watch* Republican Party Reservation. **They** *like to have sex with normal people using knives, guns, and brand new sexual organs that you did not know existed. So you vote for*

television, and everyone else, as far as your eye can see, votes to fuck you with switchblades. That's voting. You're welcome."

The sole qualm I have with this analogy is that we're not lone dissenters at the mercy of an overwhelming mob. We have numbers. If you're gay—or just a freedom-lover who wants to fight for the beaten down—then fight those who seek to pass laws against gay marriage. Don't vote against the measure because doing so is a tacit admission that voting on such matters is the proper thing to do. Instead, challenge the very notion that such things should be voted on. If you can't win on that basis, then it's time to get more extreme. For my own legal safety I can't tell you what extremes you might go to to preserve freedom, but I'll tell you what Thomas Jefferson had to say about it. *"The tree of liberty must be refreshed from time to time with the blood of patriots and tyrants. It is its natural manure."*

Commercials For Mediocrity

Television has taught me much about my enemy, the human race. It has shown me, with stark clarity, their every perverse desire and oppressive insecurity. It has lain naked before me their cruelty and ignorance. One drunken night, I sat before this idiot box—what Harlan Ellison in his infinite insight into all things dubbed "the glass teat"—with a pen in hand and a notebook sprawled out on the coffee table before me, jotting down the messages of television advertisements in the most undiluted terms I could manage. Here is a sampling of the results:

1. Save money on car insurance with *Progressive*, so that you can waste it on frivolous purchases that your wife doesn't know about.

2. If you play the game "*Rock Band*" for the *Nintendo Wii*, you will become as cool as the members of an actual band.

3. Anything that you do after midnight, other than going to *Denny's*, will turn out badly.

4. *Red Bull Energy Drink* will enable you to fly to Heaven for the purpose of exacting revenge on your recently deceased husband for leaving his fortune to his mistress rather than you and the two children you had with him.

5. Attractive people are all inexplicably using dating services, so your ugly ass had better get in on that action.

6. Penis Enlargement Pill (*Extenz*) is "scientifically proven" and if it didn't work then its makers could not possible afford to put commercials for it on television.

7. Without a drug called *ProGene*, you will be a completely unsatisfactory lover. Graphs are presented to prove this fact.

8. With *AutoZone*, you can restore a shitty old car that you found on the side of the road to working condition if you work on it constantly for months on end.

Let's examine these concepts one-by-one and extrapolate their appeal, shall we? We shall.

1. Save money on car insurance with *Progressive*, so that you can waste it on frivolous purchases that your wife doesn't know about.

Saving money is obviously desirable, but not good enough to really sell insurance in *Progressive's* opinion. You also have to spell out for people what they could do with this money and, in this instance, they're saying, "Hey guy's, with all the money you'll save you could buy shit behind your wife's back! She'll never find out!"

Only a fool would look to commercials for their morality and obviously no one looks at this material as though it were meant to influence or persuade us—but it is and it does!

If commercials didn't persuade us to buy products, then multi-billion-dollar corporations would not waste money utilizing them to sell everything from car insurance to low-fat yogurt. Why then is it a stretch to think that this message of, "It's okay—or at least expected—to go behind your wife's back with the household's finances" might be influential?

2. If you play the game "*Rock Band*" for the *Nintendo Wii*, you will become as cool as the members of an actual band.

The oldest lie in the advertiser's arsenal: X will make you cool. You must have X. Without X your life will be reduced to a hideous montage of shame and degradation.

What most uncool people never seem to realize, even under the crushing weight of all those unfulfilled promises of thousands upon thousands of products designed to make you cool, is that cool simply isn't sold in a store. A loser in a corvette parked outside his palatial estate is still a loser. If this inescapable truth was ever realized, the entire advertising industry would be destroyed overnight.

And *that* would be fucking cool.

3. Anything that you do after midnight, other than going to *Denny's*, will turn out badly.

This is a strange phenomena of recent advertising: the non sequitur masquerading as conventional wisdom. You haven't always known that everything you do after midnight is doomed to fail? Well, you've always known it now.

As soon as Denny's creates this conventional wisdom, they immediately defy it! How bold! "Marvel at how we stand in defiance of the principle that we ourselves contrived for the specific purpose of boldly defying it!"

4. *Red Bull Energy Drink* will enable you to fly to Heaven for the purpose of exacting revenge on your recently deceased husband for leaving his fortune to his mistress rather than you and the two children you had with him.

I like commercials that make claims that are so ridiculous that they are designed to not be believed. Energy drinks in particular enjoy this technique. A man drinks a *Vault* and he suddenly has the ability to punch out sharks while clubbing lesser men to death with his erect penis.

Why is this commercial making the claim that the product it advertises can do things that even the dumbest viewer knows with a binding certainty it cannot do? I think it's to distract us from the fact that the product doesn't actually do anything.

5. Attractive people are all inexplicably using dating services, so your ugly ass had better get in on that action.

Is there even one among us who really believes this? People—men in particular—are so controlled by their sexual organs that many advertisers wisely choose to ignore their brains altogether. Will men who know damn well that attractive women don't use telephone dating services suspend their disbelief long enough to cough up a credit card number? You and I both know the answer.

6. Penis Enlargement Pill (*Extenz*) is "scientifically proven" and if it didn't work then its makers could not possible afford to put commercials for it on television.

What I adore most about this commercial is its shaky attempt at logic. Rarely does a commercial attempt to employ logic—even of the shaky variety—so one has to give them a measure of credit for their attempt.

7. Without a drug called *ProGene*, you will be a completely unsatisfactory lover. Graphs are presented to prove this fact.

They've got charts! How could anyone ever possibly resist the fact-laden persuasive power of a brightly colored pie chart insisting their urgent need for a particular product?

Actually, how could anyone not resist that?

8. With *AutoZone*, you can restore a shitty old car that you found on the side of the road to working condition if you work on it constantly for months on end.

This commercial really touched my heart. A teenage boy finds a dilapidated car on the side of the road with a note in the window that reads "If you can fix it you can have it." So the boy gets a job and works his butt off until he has all the parts he needs to slowly repair the car. His tenacity and resolve exemplify the American Spirit!

As does his stupidity.

He spent his summer getting parts to fix a shitty car that someone abandoned on the side of the road when he could have just saved up to buy a used car already in working condition.

So, what can we extrapolate from these commercials? I won't force any conclusions on you, but here's the conclusion that I'm forcing on you: human beings, especially Americans, are the most gullible assortment of rubes to ever walk this shit-covered ball of filth and bacteria that we call Earth.

Now, this may strike you as unfair and unreasonable, and I will concede that it is.

However, it also happens to be true.

Our Heroes

Our heroes are not scientists or explorers. Challenge an American on the streets to name 10 scientists off the top of his head. Ask them if they know the name of even one current astronaut. Watch them fumble stupidly.

Our heroes are not artists. We might lovingly embrace a director or a singer every now and then, but usually only if they're directing movies about exploding trucks[24] or singing about how great America is and how much they like expensive things and sexual intercourse.

Our heroes are not actors and actresses. We've turned them into our public freakshow, putting the pressure of our intense scrutiny on them and then waiting for them to snap under the weight of our merciless judgment.

Our heroes are not everyday people like us. We're a bunch of fat, complacent slobs. We'd be idiots to admire one another.

We pay a little bit of lip-service to firemen and police and soldiers—but at the end of the day those people have no impact on most of us (other than those cited in vague allusions to "keeping us safe" and "fighting for our freedom").

If you think soldiers and firemen are our real heroes than ask why so many homeless people are veterans. Ask why firemen don't get multi-million dollar endorsement deals. Ask why you've never seen a panel of guys sitting around a table talking about

---

[24] I'm looking at you, Michael fucking Bay.

their favorite fireman or how amazing a certain cop's takedown of a particular criminal was.

But there are two factions of people in America these days. There are those who have heroes and those who have to act as if they do not. I will write about the latter first and segue into a discussion of the former from there.

A lot of my friends, whom I consider to be among the smarter living denizens of shitball #3[25], say that they have no heroes. I view this as partly a response to the inanity of what is considered heroic in modern America and partly a consequence of the look-up-to-no-one trend started by Kurt Cobain in the early 90's. Kurt was a reaction to the ridiculously flashy and fake rockstars dominating the scene at the end of the 80's—guys gallivanting around in yellow spandex and purple codpieces, wailing like banshees about rocking your body and touching your body and tasting your body and doing a whole assortment of other unseemly things to your body. With Kurt, the idea of the rockstar as a God-like figure who was simply better and cooler than you in every possible way went to its grave. The rockstar was now just an everyday guy—perhaps with a bit more poetry in his or her soul, but otherwise indistinguishable from the masses. Playing a gig in jeans and a T-shirt was now not only okay, it was expected. Dressing up in flamboyant costumes was now looked upon as the behavior of a poser.

Since then, those rules have been relaxed to admit more

---

[25] Sometimes referred to as Earth.

theatrical acts like Marilyn Manson and Slipknot into the darker bowels of the mainstream—but as oft-derided acts taken seriously only by their hardcore fans and laughed off by most others.

When we look for the ultimate fulfillment of our most closely held values—we can only ever see them perfectly realized within the world of fiction. In movies and films and even (for some of us) books there exists a moral simplicity that is innately gratifying.

In film, Batman was transformed from a campy crime-fighter in tights in 1966 to a rich boy out for a good time bullying criminals in 1989 to a brooding bad ass with an unbreakable will in 2008. The trend here was towards a more human rendition of the character. Adam West's Batman was silly, Michael Keaton's was dull and spoiled, Christian Bale's was complex and believable.

By now some of you are wondering what the hell I'm rambling about, so I'll spell it out: our heroes are becoming people who don't want to be our heroes. Is there any doubt that Axl Rose loves nothing more than being loved and adored and worshipped by whatever remains of his pathetic fan-base? Kurt Cobain, on the other hand, felt deeply conflicted about the idea of being a role model. He didn't really feel up to the task of being anyone's hero. Christian Bale and Christopher Nolan crafted a similar Batman—one who felt unworthy of being a hero and unsure if he could handle the pressures of being perceived as such.

For this reason, the no-heroes crowd respectfully pretends to not have heroes. Even if they adore the ever-loving shit out of someone, they act as though they don't to spare their heroes a little bit of the pressure of being heroes. It's awful considerate of them really.

The pro-heroes crowd is not so considerate, but their heroes don't want them to be. The heroes of pro-heroes people are typically self-absorbed athletes with more muscles than brains. It is always fun to watch as these heroes are fed a steady diet of love from the public for years and years, feeding their already morbidly obese egos, until one day some fact about them comes to light or they start to lose their game and their sycophantic devotees evaporate like a mirage. That's when the tabloids and the gossip shows (and, increasingly, the actual news) get ahold of them. The Green Goblin from 2002's Spiderman was among the lamest realizations of an iconic comic book villain in cinematic history, but I always found myself agreeing with his contention that the one thing people love more than a hero is to see a hero fall.

And before your criticize me for referencing superheroes twice in one section, I'd remind you that I'm about as nerdy as a person can be. As a teenager, acne accounted for more of my body mass than penis did. Besides, this is a chapter about heroes—and super ones are the most idealized of all.

This notion, by the way, fits perfectly into my idea that athletes are our ultimate heroes. Who could ever be more athletic than superheroes? They can run faster than speeding bullets and leap tall buildings in a single bound! The superheroes are the home team and all the supervillains are from rival schools. It fits together eerily well—at least in my mind.

I don't know if we can choose our heroes or if who we admire is inexorably linked to our own values—wherever those are derived from—but it seems to me that we should have deep admiration for anyone who is especially talented at what they do. Why can't a man who can eat more hotdogs than most people be a small-time hero? My stepfather is an excellent contractor and carpenter—why does that skill entitle him to less hero worship than a guy who can pluck a guitar well? Don't we need roofs over our heads and four walls to hold them up as much as we need music to reverberate off of those walls?

Am I being too idealistic? I had better stop in that case.

Sorrow & Flatulence

"TJ, there's something seriously wrong with your father."

I'd be lying if I said panic was my first reaction to those words. The sentence, and its meaning, made the room I was occupying seem larger. It made me feel smaller.

I rose from my chair, jogged briskly to the bedroom where my father lay moaning inhumanly. His face was purple, his eyes glassy.

We turned him over. His beige pants were drenched with urine. "Oh god," shouted my stepmom. "He's pissed himself."

At that moment, we all knew he was going to die.

It was the unspoken obvious fact that filled the room like a cloud of noxious gas. "Oh god, he's pissed himself" was grief-stricken wife speak for: "Of fuck, he's a goner!"

We—me, my brother and my stepmom—managed to get him onto the floor. She pumped his chest and blew into his mouth. I called 9-1-1. The breaths she gave him seemed to bypass his lungs entirely, simply inflating his stomach instead. They came out in little bursts of cartoonish snoring that would have sounded funny under different circumstances. Hell, they're kind of funny even in retrospect, albeit in a dark and haunting way.

Paramedics arrived quickly and worked on him for what seemed liked 15-minutes but was probably a considerable shorter period of time. They managed to restore his pulse. They were all very casual. It was nothing they hadn't seen a hundred times before--just another family destroyed, just another person sucked into oblivion, just another day at work.

I freely admit to hating them to this day, despite knowing that detachment is an important part of their job.

We stewed in the hospital's waiting room while doctors performed surgery. We were told that my father had suffer a massive heart-attack.

The waiting room was filled with people wanting to be seen for minor illnesses. A black woman kept shouting how outrageous it was that she had to wait so long for treatment for her sickle-cell. "I know these white people in here ain't got no sickle-cell!" she shouted indignantly. I wanted to smash her face into the brick wall that I was leaning on as I sat on the floor because stupid cretinous morons like her had taken all the chairs. I wanted to pound her face into a pulp until sickle-cell was at the very bottom of her list of medical problems.

Being in the hospital that night kicked killed the conservative in me. Not all at once, but it was the first blow to all my high-minded idealism about the strong pulling themselves up by their bootstraps. Here I was, surrounded by the weak—the poor, the infirm, the refuge of society. I had an epiphany then (though it was drowned by grief): these people were my countrymen. These sickly people and these relatives of sickly people were my fellow human beings. That hard truth is that no one is strong. We are all fundamentally weak because no matter how spectacular we may fancy ourselves to be, we're still biological organisms of immense frailty.

My friend Logan was driving in a car with his girlfriend once and he had to slam on the brakes to avoid a collision. His girlfriend wasn't wearing her seatbelt and her head smacked against the windshield. She was largely unharmed, but Logan realized that if he hadn't hit the brakes when he had, he'd have crashed and she would have been severely injured or worse. He told me then how he hated the fragility of human life.

There was a time when I would have agreed with him, and much of me still does. However, and in spite of all the sorrow it has caused me and countless other human beings, I kind of dig our fragility. Marilyn Manson, who just so happens to be the most brilliant man on earth, puts it best in his song "The Reflecting God":

> *Without the threat of death*
> *There's no reason to live at all*

Isn't that the truest statement ever spoken or sung? Without death, life has no meaning. Existence is no fun if it's not temporary. That's why we drive too fast, do drugs, eat shitty food and all that fun stuff. We like to give death a big middle finger and dare him to bite us in the ass.

But I digress.

I was in the hospital room waiting for my father to get out of surgery. Everyone knew he was going to die. There were no delusions. We were all attempting to lie to ourselves, but none of us believed our own bullshit. Maybe if he'd contracting cancer or something like that and we'd had weeks to lie to ourselves instead of just hours, we could have tricked ourselves. That wasn't the case though.

I supposed that the first time a loved one dies, you should come away with a deeper understanding of yourself. It's sort of expected of you. "My dad died, but I gained such and such insight into myself." It's our way of acting like us and the world are Even Steven. So, without further delay, here are somethings I learned about myself in exchange for my fathers death.

GRAND ISIGHT INTO MYSELF #1: I fart a lot when I'm consumed by grief and shock and terror.

I could scarcely go a minute without releasing the most rank and vile farts known to man. I was in a room filled with sick people, waiting for news about my father's fate and I was farting. Nothing in those overwrought dramatic films about personal tragedy prepares you for such incongruities. Sorrow and flatulence are supposed to be mutually exclusive occurrences.

Farting while be dad was dying taught me this: there is no "supposed to be" in the real world. Reality doesn't care about "ought" or "should." Hoping, praying, wishing, expecting—these activities are akin to wading up a piece of paper and throwing it at a tank.

GRAND ISIGHT INTO MYSELF #2: I have a thick country accent when I'm bereaved.

I stood beside my father's deathbed with my normally unaffectionate brother clinging to me as if I was the sole thing keeping him from spiraling into madness. I spoke to my father for the last time—knowing full well that he couldn't hear or perceive a goddamn thing that I said. I may as well have been talking to a wall.

I begged him—in a thick southern accent that I don't normally have—to pull a miracle out of his ass. I told him that if anyone could defy the odds it was him. I swore that if he made a full recovery, I—an atheist since childhood—would praise whatever God may be in any way that I could.

Hours later, he was dead.

The nurses told us that he had no chance and that even if he survived he would likely have serious brain damage. I said, "That's not what he'd want," and I had them take him off the machines that were keeping him alive.

It was amazing how quickly he went from a human being to a corpse. His body was suddenly so stiff and lifeless. When I gave him my departing hug, it felt as though I were hugging a mannequin or a wax figure.

I went home that night and the first thing I did was make a YouTube video[26]. It may seem peculiar, but I've never been one

---

[26] http://www.youtube.com/watch?v=Bo-q7RgABIg

to suffer in the shadows. I want people to know that I'm in pain—just like I want them to know when I'm angry or happy. I always want everyone to share in my emotional state[27].

The night my father died taught me a number of important things. It taught me that I fart a lot under stress. It taught me that I have a thick southern accent when I get really upset. It taught me that no matter how full of life someone seems, they may be close to death.

Most importantly, it taught me that life isn't fair. We're told that all the time growing up. I couldn't possibly count the number of times I was told as a child that life isn't fair—but I didn't really realize it until I was 23 and my father died before ever even getting to wear the watch I bought him for Christmas. Oh well. Life goes on. . . .

Until it doesn't.

---

[27] It is this trend in my behavior, more than anything else about me, that makes writing vital to my existence. Plenty of people have told me that I lack talent, that I have a tin ear for language—they act as though this means something or is someone a point. I write because I can't go through life without putting words down.

Bitches Be Crazy

So there's this girl. . . .

I wonder how many stories start that way. I'm betting that most of the stories men tell start with some variation of those words. Love stories start that way, hate stories start that way; tales of everything from redemption to obsession start with "a girl."

Girls are capable of an intensity of emotions that most men could never muster. Any man who has ever argued with a girl knows this. Reason and logic are thrown out the window the moment that a girl's feelings are hurt.

Some will call these sentiments sexist, and rightfully so—because they are. This has little bearing, however, on my subject matter for this chapter. I have a little bit of a story to tell you, and in telling you this story I hope to prove a point about gender and about America. Failing that, I hope to amuse you with a tale of obsessive behavior. Gather 'round children and allow me to tell you a story. It starts like this:

So there's this girl named Gwen. That's short for Gwendolyn but that doesn't really matter since Gwen is not her real name.

She's an overweight teenage vegan who dreams of being famous. She is straight edge[28] but is considering quitting so that she can do cocaine. She greets people by saying, "Wanna get a

---
[28] Someone who doesn't do drugs because they're a pussy.

pizza and fuck?" Her mother is a lesbian social-worker. She is obsessed with Vanilla Ice. She yells at people when they eat eggs because it's animal cruelty. She hates all the girls that like me because they like me. She brings up interesting topics in passing and then discusses boring ones at length. She frequently alludes to fantasies wherein I have sex with my brother or my friend Cody for her pleasure. She has Charles Manson eyes and gigantic tits. She will IM me for hours solid even if I don't IM her back even once. She alternately tells me that she watches all my videos and tells me that she's only watched two or three of them. She thinks the Columbine killers are cute. She thinks she's a good person, but she does not value human life. She hates me one day and loves me the next.

She is unaware of most of these traits.

I've told her that she is a crazy bitch. I've called her dirt. I've been as mean as possible to her. I've talked to her in ways that would have driven some people to take a razor to their wrists—and she's taken no offense. Other days I have vaguely alluded, in the politest possible term, to strange idiosyncrasies in her personality and reduced her to tears and rage.

She asks me for advice at times. She is terrified of the future. She doesn't want to be an adult. She fears that it will be more difficult to make friends, even though she has no friends. She fears that adults don't have enough sex, though she doesn't have any now. She's essentially afraid that adulthood will be different by being exactly the same.

When I was a kid only my gay uncle ever told me the truth about being an adult. When I asked 99% of adults what it was like to be a grown-up they'd tell me that it was awful and that I'd better enjoy my childhood while it lasted. My gay uncle didn't bother with that smokescreen. "Being an adult is way better," he said. "You don't have to put up with a bunch of people telling you what to do all the time. You can sit around in your living room in your underwear with a joint and a bowl of soup and no one gives a fuck."

So I essentially told Gwen the same thing, but for her it seemed like a nightmare. I asked her then, "What are you afraid of Gwen?" The following is her exact answer:

"Getting an obsession, not getting married, not having anyone fall in love with me, spiders, having kids with worse mental problems than me, being fat the rest of my life, not being successful, my cat dying before me, never being "hot", my agent (she scares the shit out of me), people who are really nice to me to the point I don't know if they're real, being dependant on my meds, not getting into college, and ketchup."

It's hard not to pity someone with so many fears. I felt a tinge of sympathy for her. I have my moments of humanity[29].

Then I began to wonder, "Do I even have the right to by sympathetic?" I'm as obsessive as she is and I fear that no one will ever love me. I'm scared of having kids even more fucked up then me. I'm scared of not being successful. I worry about my sick dog.

---

[29] Well, not really. But it makes for better writing.

I distrust overly nice people and view them as phonies.

I don't fear spiders or ketchup. Hell, I'd eat spider in Ketchup is someone offered it up as an exotic dish. I don't take any meds, though I arguably ought to.

Most of the fears that make her seem pathetic to me are fears that I share. The traits I hate most are ones I share most.

Is my sending angry letters to a girl I broke up with 5-years-ago any less horribly obsessive than her writing my name across her tits and sending them to me without any provocation? Is my raging at people who believe in even the least dogmatic of deities any different than her raging at people for eating eggs?

Girls.

They reflect us with an emotional rawness that we could never muster. They show us our every insecurity, magnified by an order of magnitude. They are us better than we are ourselves.

That's why we hate them. That's why we love them.

That's why Muslims put drapes over them. That's why we subtly encourage them to wear as little as possible.

Girls.

Damned elusive beasts of our hearts.[30]

---

[30] If you're a girl who just so happens to not be a lesbian, this chapter doesn't really speak to you, does it? It speaks about you, and it speaks about you as though you're not here. That has to be someone disconcerting. I apologize for that. You can have free sex with me as a consolation if you present this book to me with this footnote hi-lighted.

Similarly, if you're a gay guy who couldn't give a fuck less about girls and their mysteries, I apologize for writing an utterly inaccessible chapter. You can have free gay sex with me as a consolation if you present this book to me with this footnote hi-lighted.

Free and Dumb

Congress shall make no law respecting an establishment of religion, or prohibiting the free exercise thereof; or abridging the freedom of speech, or of the press; or the right of the people peaceably to assemble, and to petition the Government for a redress of grievances.

Today I saw a story on the news about a 15-year-old girl arrested for child pornography because she took nude pictures *of herself*[31]. In other words, the government of this country has boldly declared, yet again, that we belong to them. Our bodies are not our own to do with what we please—they are fodder for Uncle Sam's meat grinder.

We call this a free country, but everything about this country is designed to stifle freedom. Now, many conservative rednecks like the ones I live around will tell you, "Yeah, well you try protesting in the streets in China and then you'll be grateful for the freedom you got here."

That's right. According to every redneck I've ever gotten into an argument with, America is a free country because we're more free than countries like China, Russia, Iran and North Korea. That's like saying that McDonalds serves healthy food because it's not as bad for you as getting shot in the face. I like to ask these rednecks (who are by no means inherently stupid people, by the

---

[31] http://www.foxnews.com/story/0,2933,434645,00.html

way) if they've ever tried to protest here in America. Most say that they haven't. I ask them why. They say because they don't think it would change things.

Which leads me to the question that not one of them can answer sufficiently: If protesting can't change things, then why does the right to protest matter?

Of course, in America we have such a thing as Free Speech Zones,[32] which are specific places set up where protestors are allowed to demonstrate against any given thing. What's the point of a right to protest if you can't protest where those whose actions you are protesting can see and hear you? And does not the first Amendment of the Constitution of the United States of America that every government official is sworn to uphold state that all of America is a "Free Speech Zone"?

Anyone who has ever filed a Demonstration Permit—*the very concept of which makes me sick*—and seen it rejected can tell you all about your right to protest. Ask the people who protested the WTO in Seattle (it doesn't matter here if you agree with their paranoid fear of multinational conglomerates or not) how they feel about the state of their right to protest. Getting sprayed with hoses, shot with rubber bullets and tear-gassed by police in full battle regalia tends to diminish one's ideas about any sort of right to protest in America.

Exactly what freedoms do you think you have, America? The freedom to timidly voice a complaint with the way things are

---

[32] http://en.wikipedia.org/wiki/Free_speech_zones

going? The freedom to pay less in taxes than most European countries, perhaps? Take my hand for a moment (it's okay, I use sanitizer) and follow me down this road.

Poll after poll has shown the Americans of all political stripes overwhelmingly favor some form of Universal Healthcare[33], yet to watch the news you would imagine that the country was fiercely divided on this issue (and if you watch Fox News you'd get the impression that only hardcore socialists would even suggest such a thing). Does the government say, "Wow, look at those polls! We better get on this problem right away!"?

No.

Instead our representatives (HA!) say, "Wow, the private insurance industry sure is giving us a lot of money. I guess we can tell 70 to 80% of people that it's just not feasible and that they're unpatriotic for wanting it."

Here's just how stupid and controllable the electorate is: just today I overheard a redneck saying that the Democrats removed the word God from a WWII memorial. It was an excerpt from Roosevelt's speech following the attack on Pearl Harbor, and it was removed by the Godless Democrats who want to write God out of history. This set my bullshit detector off immediately and I did some research. I found that, yes, God was mentioned in Roosevelt's speech. However, the excerpt found on the memorial in question NEVER included anything about God. The aforementioned redneck was complaining that God was nowhere

---

[33] http://www.cbsnews.com/stories/2007/03/01/opinion/polls/main2528357.shtml

to be found in a sentence that God was never in. Further, he boldly declared—*as if it were a fact*—that Democrats were to blame for this "travesty."

Let me explain politics in America to you, folks. The Republicans are *Coca-Cola* and the Democrats are *Pepsi-Cola*. That's all you need to know. Same drink, for all intents and purposes. Some people will swear up and down that there are vast differences between the two—Coke people say the Pepsi has a bad aftertaste and Pepsi people say that Coke has a bad aftertaste, but if you give a Coke person a Pepsi or a Pepsi person a Coke, most can't tell the fucking difference.

The difference is all in the packaging and the marketing. It doesn't matter that these drinks taste nearly identical—to watch the competing ads for the two, you'd imagine that no two drinks were ever so different. But folks, be intelligent for a minute, two things that are genuinely different don't need to spend millions of dollars a year convincing you of how different they are. Milk doesn't put out ads telling you not to drink orange juice. *Peanut Butter Crunch* has never and will never put out an ad letting you know just how superior their cereal is to mashed potatoes and gravy.

Democrats and Republicans are essentially the same beast, and I've created a helpful flowchart that shows you how they decide policy:

[The chart no longer exists. Use your imagination]

That's the breakdown, boys and girls. The folks on CNN would love it to be more complicated than that, but it's not. Americans would like to believe that one side fights for them and the other side are ravenous monsters who want to see America's values crumble to the dirt, but that's not the case either. When you believe that, you're a puppet. The GOP or the DNC have a big greasy hand up your ass. Your lips are moving, but the words aren't coming from inside your head—they're coming from Rush Limbaugh or Michael Moore (neither of whom I have any particular problem with, by the way).

There's nothing wrong with having your own beliefs, but when you view your opponents as not just wrong, but somehow malevolent, you're not solving anything. You're not just part of the problem; you *are* the problem. If the people stopped worrying that the other half of the people were fucking them in the ass they might stop to notice that both "sides" are holding *everyone* down while the corporations fuck each and every one of us.

Now, let's be clear: I'm not advocating the destruction of corporations. I love that we're a country of mass production where I can buy a computer for less than a grand or eat at cheeseburger for 1/6th of an hour's labor at minimum wage. I like that we can get quality goods at affordable prices. What I'm not happy about—and what none of us should be happy about—is that these same corporations are ruling over our government. We did not elect Wal-Mart or Halliburton our leaders and it shouldn't be up to them whether we pass environmental reforms or labor reforms or enact economic regulations. They deserve a voice, but they don't deserve an amplifier. They don't deserve more say in the fate of the American people than the American people.

As long as they keep us fat and fatalistic, they will keep control. As long as we continue to believe that they are unstoppable, they are. As long as we worry about fake issues, we will be distracted from the important truth that we are powerless. It doesn't matter what we want. It only matters what IBM and Wachovia want.

And they don't want you to be free. They want you to be a dumb slave who will pull the cart along without question. Thusfar you've given them what they want.

What Is Freedom?

In the greatest B-movie of all time, "Deathrace 2000", Sylvester Stallone plays a character with the enviable name of Machine Gun Joe Viterbo who is introduced to a jeering arena of spectators with one of the most underrated lines in all of cinema: "Here he comes! Machine Gun Joe! Loved by thousands, hated by millions!"

That's the essence of freedom, folks.

When you're loved, you are held to a gold standard that no human being can really live up to. When you're hated, almost anything you get up to is fully expected of you. If the governor fucks a hooker, it's a story that makes the front page of all the newspapers; but if the governor's gardener fucks a hooker, it's hardly even a story to tell your friends at work.

The good man—or, at least, the man who is thought to be good—is not free to tell the truth. He has to worry about what the neighbors will think, what the papers will think, what his golf buddies will think. How will they look at him when he goes to his favorite Mexican restaurant? How will they treat him in the checkout line at the grocery store? He can't tell the truth. He can only parrot one of two or three socially acceptable positions on any given subject matter.

The bad man—or, at least, the man who is thought to be bad—is not similarly constrained. He can tell the truth all day long because he doesn't give a fuck what the neighbors think. The papers don't report what he says or does. He doesn't play any faggoty games like golf. He is used to getting nasty looks wherever he goes. He knows that people don't approve of him or the way he lives his life. He can tell the truth.

Truth is freedom. Freedom is truth.

When a boy who looked like he could be anywhere between 12 and 20 walked up to me in a crowded bookstore and said my name, I was puzzled as to who he could be or how he might know me. My first guess was that I went to school with him, but he looked far too young for that to be the case. "I watch you on YouTube," he told me, extending a hand for me to shake it.

It never occurred to me until that moment that there were actual flesh and blood human beings, who occupied the same physical realm as I did, watching my videos. It was off-putting. I was pouring my heart and soul out to actual human beings? How unlike me! It was cringe-inspiring and traumatic to think that people, no better than any people that I had ever encountered in my life, knew things about me.

Of course, on a rational level, I always knew that my audience was comprised of real human beings. I was under no illusion that my subscribers were as physically intangible as the characters that I have always created in my head. But there is a massive chasm—at least for me—between rational reality and visceral reality. It's the difference between hearing the words, "Your friend is dead" and actually seeing your friend's lifeless bullet-riddled corpse. It's the difference between what we know and what we *know*.

There is a cruelty inherent to the relatively new medium of internet vlogging in that it lures us into believing in some gullible and intellectually soft area of our brains that we are not talking to an audience, but to ourselves. By the time we realize otherwise—truly realize it—we're already exposed.

From that initial sting of realization, there can only come relief. It's a relief most people will never experience—the relief of being freed from the burden of the mask of their own contrived banality. Once you've opened your mouth and removed all doubt that you are a complete nutjob, you don't have to pretend otherwise anymore.

Truth is freedom. Freedom is truth.

On September 11th 2001, this entire nation was awestruck with the spectacle of an attack on American soil of proportions not seen since December 7th, 1941. The American people rightly screamed for justice. They wanted to see those responsible for the heinous act against their fellow American's punished.

That's the problem with suicide attackers. You can't retaliate against them. They're already dead.

This is probably why so many Americans called the 9/11 hijackers cowards in the wake of the attacks, but by now we can all surely set that comforting lie aside and admit to ourselves that cowards do not die in the pursuit of their goals. The hijackers were certainly evil, brain-washed idiots—but not cowards. They were, in fact, bold and brave men who made the ultimate sacrifice for what they believed in.

The bloodlust of the American populace could not be sated with the destruction of those who perpetrated the attack against us, because it was a destruction that they had chosen for themselves. We had to go after who they worked for, and instead of investigating the matter thoroughly, the Bush administration pinned it exclusively on Osama Bin Laden and the Taliban in Afghanistan, ignoring the ties of almost all of the hijackers to Saudi Arabia.

Soon enough, even Osama was forgotten. The war in Afghanistan was swallowed alive by the war in Iraq. The bloodlust of the American people formed a red carpet for big government and big business to stroll into the Middle East and set up shop. Military contractors like Vice President Dick Cheney's former employer Halliburton made record profits by overcharging the government for busy work. Oil Companies like Exxon made record profits while gas prices nearly quadrupled. By the time Americans forgot about their need for vengeance, they found themselves stuck in a war that will end up costing nearly a trillion dollars and has already cost thousands of lives.

If these were the events of a novel, you'd be incensed if the fictional population of the book didn't revolt and overthrow their government for such a miscarriage of their will. But this isn't a tidy fiction, it is a complex reality and the American people are too stupid and defeated to have the means or the inclination to rebel against their masters.

So, the question becomes: How did a population descended from a bunch of badass rebels who kicked the ever-loving shit out of the English when King George III tried to tax them too highly turn into a cluster of tepid pussies with no real ambition? How did the home of the free and the land of the brave become the land of the timid and the home of the enslaved?

The American people were tamed by a trifecta of factors: safety, patriotism and individualism. Now, I happen to believe that safety, patriotism and individualism are good things. However, when those who run the system use these concepts, they use them as weapons against the people. Safety starts to mean fear. Patriotism starts to mean obedience. Individualism starts to mean lack of empathy.

Safety is a good thing. There's no reason for people to be needlessly endangered. The thing is, safety is not something that should trump personal freedom—as it did when our government passed The Patriot Act.

Patriotism is a good thing. When you take pride in your country, you want to see it prosper. You want to make sure it is a peaceful and opportunity-rich place for the next generation to inherit. However, when patriotism is transformed into blind support for one's government, then it ceases to be a force for positivity and instead becomes a detriment to that which we should most cherish. Our children do not benefit from a world where corporate profit is king. The mindless obedience of the populace to the idea that corporate greed is good does not feel like patriotism to me. It feels a damn sight more like treason.

Individualism is certainly a good thing, but when individualism turns into the notion of "every man for himself" then it is a basically Social Darwinism. You see this mentality reflected in the inability of the American public to forgive any transgression. If a politician sleeps with a prostitute, they want him to resign. If a man kills another man in the heat of passion, people want him to go to jail for the rest of his life. If a man molests a child, instead of trying to find out why this urge exists and making an effort to prevent it from occurring in the future, the people call for his head on a stick.

The fork whose prongs are safety, patriotism and individualism has been stuck into us and we're done. This triplet doctrine has rendered the free and the brave into a great and huddling mass of selfish slaves who take orders because they're too fearful to ask questions and too uncertain to make demands.

Too often, those who maintain courage and freedom and true individuality attempt to free the people by simply addressing the symptoms of the disease of servitude to the system. This is not effective. We must eliminate the disease itself.

This can be done be educating the populace as to the true meanings of the virtues of safety, patriotism and individuality.

Safety does not just mean death-prevention. Human beings are not the only things that need to be kept safe. It is also important—more so, in fact—to keep the noble aspects of human beings alive. Freedom of choice, freedom of association, freedom from unreasonable taxation, freedom of and from religion, freedom to dissent—these things must be kept safe too.

And who would really wish to live in a world of absolute safety? We can make people safer by taking away all their rights just like we can make the streets safer by outlawing cars. That doesn't make it a good idea.

Patriotism should be pride taken in the accomplishments of our society. When we have a good economy and a surplus of freedoms, it is good to look upon that wealth and freedom and say, "this is good shit!" Patriotism also means recognizing faults with the system and coming up with solutions to fix them.

I have a deep and profound love for my country, but in times like these it's a bit like being in love with a crack whore who you know will steal your stereo and sell it for crack if you fall asleep with her in your house. We shouldn't let America sell our stereos for crack. It's not right.

Individualism means being true to yourself, not being a slave to self-interest. Let me give you an example of what I mean, since I know that a good deal of my Libertarian readers are currently scratching their heads and saying to themselves, "but that's not what Ayn Rand said!"

The American right-wing is fond of the buzzwords "personal responsibility." If you've ever watched Glenn Beck (I don't recommend it), you'd think it was the name for the Philosopher's Stone. He can hardly let a sentence pass by without throwing "personal responsibility" into it.

Ask yourself: "What exactly is personal responsibility?" It's the idea that no matter what happens in your life, it is entirely your fault and entirely your problem. If there is a housing crisis and you were the victim of predatory lending practices, it's your fault for not understanding the legal jargon that you signed before your Mortgage tripled. If you were drunk at a bar and a man grabbed your girlfriend's ass and you punched him and he fell and hit his head on hard on the floor and died, you're a murderer and you should go to prison for the rest of your life. If you are a 25-year-old man and you start flirting with a girl and take her back to your apartment and fuck her in every hole she's got . . . only to later discover that she was 14, guess what? You're a pedophile and you'll go to prison, get your ass beat and buggered on a daily basis until eventually they'll let you out, make you go to a shrink and put you on a list that ensures you'll never hold another good job and you won't be able to live pretty much anywhere.

Personal responsibility in action, folks.

It's been misapplied to the point of uselessness. Of course people should be responsible for the things they do, but we as a people have somehow come to the conclusion that this means that no one is ever allowed to make a mistake or have a moment of weakness. We are a bunch of unforgiving douchebags, and the reason for it is because Mr. A doesn't care if Mr. B goes to prison on some bogus charges. And guess what? Mr. C won't give a shit when Mr. B goes to prison a few weeks later on the same charge.

America has the highest incarceration rate in the world.

THE. HIGHEST. IN. THE. WORLD.

Here in the land of the free, a full 1% of our population is in prison. 2 million people are incarcerated in the prison system of the United States of America.

Those in power know that we won't stand up for one another, so they can put anyone behind bars that they want. Drug-users, political dissidents, the mentally ill—anyone that can fit into a cell can be sold into slavery in this nation.

Why has this happened? Where did we go wrong? Did we forget that *truth is freedom and freedom is truth?*

What then, is truth? Ayn Rand, that sour husk of a woman whose soul was as barren as her cunt was unfuckably grotesque, once said that "A is A." If she'd had a better understanding of the mechanisms by which we perceive what we call reality she would have said "A is, for all intents a purposes, A."

She sought to make everything an objective truth, and in doing so came to a false conclusion about the nature of freedom. Her idea of freedom was a world wherein everyone was "objective" and therefore behaved in an "objective" manner.

A world where everyone thinks and acts the same is not freedom. Such a world is a planet of slaves. This is why Ayn Rand has the pseudo-Lovecraftian moniker of TBCITU (The Biggest Cunt In The Universe) in my mind.

The truth is that there is no truth.

Everything is viewed through human bias. We call the sun

hot because it's hot to us—but the sun isn't hot to itself and all the elements that make it up. Hot is our bias. Hot is subjective. Hard is subjective. Fast is subjective. Everything that makes up our seemingly solid world of airtight absolutes is entirely subjective.

Does this mean that all truth is ultimately subjective? I wouldn't say that, but I think that objective truth is so far beyond our grasp (and so far removed from our hearts) that it is essentially irrelevant.

I think that "sunsets are beautiful" is every bit as true as "the sun is hot." I think that "sunsets are ugly" is every bit as true as "sunsets are beautiful." I think that freedom is found in the ability of contradictory ideas to coexist.

A nation on non-drug-users who all believe in drugs rights would be a free nation. A nation of heterosexuals who allowed gays to have equal rights regardless of how they felt about gay people is a free nation. A nation of vanilla people who allow the kinky people to be who they are, regardless of how they feel about the kinky people's lifestyles is a free nation.

Freedom is truth. Truth is paradox.

The New Slaves

A man said to me once that the reason that so many minorities turn to lives of crime is because of gansta rap and movies that portray the criminal lifestyle as glamorous. Certainly, that may be a factor, but it's not a problem for the reason he seemed to think it was. The problem is that minorities are stupid.

Whoa. Hold on. I'm not making any sort of argument about race-based intelligence, as I find such arguments repugnant. I'm simply saying that minorities are statistically more likely to be impoverished and tend to live in areas where the schools are underfunded. Shitty education creates shitty people who make shitty parents who fail to instill within their children any sort of principles. It's no wonder that so many of these kids either grow up to perpetuate the shitty parenting cycle by producing offspring of their own or wind up initiated into gangs.

And since the crime rate is so catastrophically high in many minority areas, there are fewer small businesses operating there and therefore fewer jobs. Often times, the only means of making money is to sell drugs or steal[34].

The whole thing forms a vicious cycle that is incapable of endings without the intervention of an outside force of some kind. Violence and theft begets poverty and poverty begets violence and theft.

Now, some will choose to play their little tough guy

---

[34] Sometimes to eat, but often just to pay for drug habits.

routines and give us all that slow-clap speech about personal responsibility and toss in some crowd-pleasing snide and sarcastic "boo-hoos" that mock rather than address the problem—but that is beneath us. Or at least it should be.

Minorities are stupid due largely to the racist policies that have dominated the vast majority of American history, so of course they view what is only intended as escapism (gangsta rap, gangster movies) as guidebooks for how to live the easy life. It's natural enough that they would view that as the pinnacle of human achievement when it is essentially the glorification of the reality that they already inhabit out of necessity. Who doesn't dream of being the best at what they do? Of course every two-bit drug dealer in the Ghetto will watch *Scarface* with envious eyes. Tony Montana is a better drug dealer than him. Tony Montana is the drug dealer he wishes he was.

Art may encourage us in our chosen paths in life, but rarely does it set us upon them. More often, art is about learning to accept a circumstance or to escape into a better version of your own life than it is about making you into something that you're not. No straight-A student from a wealthy family decided to become a drug dealer just because it looks fun[35].

This hopeless cycle is made all the more horrible by the fact that it has served—by design or by happenstance—the purposes of an elite group of Americans.

The United States (*laaaaand of the freeeee*) has less than

---

[35] Well, actually, some probably do, but they're the exception, not the rule.

5 percent of the world's population, but it accounts for nearly 25% of the world's prison population[36]. If you're reading that and you're not outraged, then your sole focus in life should be to avoid breeding at all costs, because the world doesn't need more idiots like you.

Was it always like this? Were we always so fond of our "lock 'em up and throw away the key" philosophy of crime and punishment?

Since 1970, our prison population has increased by 700%[37]. You're not reading that wrong. It has literally become 8 times larger in just 38 years. (HINT: The US Population has only grown by about 30-40% in that time—statistically negligible in the face of our previous number.)

Hey, TJ, what year was the War on Drugs instituted again?

I'm glad you ask, my child. It was instituted in 1972.

But, TJ, now that we've put these violent criminals in prison, crime in this country has gone down! So the war on drugs is working! Yay!

WRONG. Most scientific evidence suggests that there is little if any relationship between fluctuations in crime rates and incarceration rates. In many cases, crime rates have risen or declined independent of imprisonment rates. New York City, for example, has produced one of the nation's largest declines in

---

[36] http://en.wikipedia.org/wiki/Prisons_in_the_United_States
[37] http://www.dailykos.com/story/2007/2/15/114022/882

crime in the nation while significantly reducing its jail and prison populations. Connecticut, New Jersey, Ohio, and Massachusetts have also reduced their prison populations during the same time that crime rates were declining.

The next question on our agenda is why are recidivism rates so abysmally and staggeringly high? First of all, let's take a look at exactly how high these rates are:

Of the 272,111 persons released from prisons in 15 States in 1994, an estimated 67.5% were rearrested for a felony or serious misdemeanor within 3 years, 46.9% were reconvicted, and 25.4% resentenced to prison for a new crime.

These are inexcusably bad results and when compared to the recidivism rates of most countries. Sweden, for instance, has a recidivism rate of only 22%! Could it be that they're doing something right and that we're doing something wrong?

Instead of seeking to punish, Swedish prisons seek to reform. Psychologists have told us for years that punishment is ineffective as a deterrent, but we as a nation continue to think we know better than what mere scientists have to say! We've got something better than science—we've got a gut instinct, a whole lot of hatred and a serious lack of empathy for our fellow man. We don't care that punishment is ineffective, because it feels so goddamn good. Vengeance is a lot more fun than being rational and trying to come up with humane solutions that treat our prisoners as human beings with inherent dignity who are no less human than us regardless of their wrong-doing.

Now, an estimated 11.9 percent of black men were in prison or jails, compared with 3.9 percent of Hispanic males and 1.7 percent of white males. The prison population in America contains many blacks and quite a few Hispanics and even a pretty decent number of white people.

These people are the new slaves in America, and it's especially sad in the instance of the blacks, who have already gone through so much. The Thirteenth Amendment to the United States Constitution, which ended one form of slavery, also codified another. "Neither slavery nor involuntary servitude, **except as a punishment for crime whereof the party shall have been duly convicted**, shall exist within the United States, or any place subject to their jurisdiction."

Prison is big business here in America. Prisoners are forced to manufacture everything from body armor for the military to the oven in your house.[38] Ever called a customer service representative for a big corporation that you had dealings with? You might have been talking to a convict. Prisons in several state contain call centers that handle calls for many big

---

[38] According to the Left Business Observer, the federal prison industry produces 100% of all military helmets, ammunition belts, bullet-proof vests, ID tags, shirts, pants, tents, bags, and canteens. Along with war supplies, prison workers supply 98% of the entire market for equipment assembly services; 93% of paints and paintbrushes; 92% of stove assembly; 46% of body armor; 36% of home appliances; 30% of headphones/microphones/speakers; and 21% of office furniture. Airplane parts, medical supplies, and much more: prisoners are even raising seeing-eye dogs for blind people.
SOURCE: http://www.politicalaffairs.net/article/view/2024/1/124/

companies[39].

Aside from being a cheap source of labor for big companies, the increasing prison population also gives politicians an opportunity to funnel tax dollars into the pockets of the contractors who build the prisons that exist to house the influx of new inmates.

According to cultural historian H. Bruce Franklin, "in the typical American prison, designed and run to maximize degradation, brutalization, and punishment, overt torture is the norm. Beatings, electric shock, prolonged exposure to heat and even immersion in scalding water, sodomy with riot batons, nightsticks, flashlights, and broom handles, shackled prisoners forced to lie in their own excrement for hours or even days, months of solitary confinement, rape and murder by guards or prisoners instructed by guards—all are everyday occurrences in the American prison system."[40]

I was skeptical of these claims myself at first, so I did a bit more digging and discovered that the internet is a veritable treasure trove of sites detailing countless specific instances of the abuse of power by guards against inmates and by inmates against one another with either the encouragement or apathy of the guards. I suggest that anyone wanting to learn more about this type the words "American prison torture" into *Google* and start clicking links.

---

[39] http://www.usatoday.com/money/economy/employment/2004-07-06-call-center_x.htm

[40] http://www.historiansagainstwar.org/resources/torture/brucefranklin.html#N_4_

So, if American prisoners are mostly minorities who are mostly poor and they are forced into labor and tortured by sadistic guards—then I can't draw any conclusion other than that these people are slaves and we are all complicit in their slavery.

Right now, as you read this sentence, a little boy is being born in a big ugly building with a name like "Community Hospital." His mother is a drug addict of some sort and he will be born with withdrawals. He will grow up without a father and with a mother more interested in scoring drugs than raising him. The schools he attends will be under-funded and he will most likely drop out. He is likely to join a gang. He is likely to go to jail. He is likely to assemble ovens or body armor for large corporations against his will.

There is a little boy being born right now that has a good chance of becoming a slave whose labor you may one day exploit. He's taking his first breath of this worlds air and he's cold and naked and he has no awareness yet of any of this.

If you find his fate tragic, don't. It hasn't happened yet—and maybe under your watch and mine, it won't have to. Demand from your politicians that our prisons be reformed and our schools along with them. Don't settle for vague promises of some nebulous coming greatness, but instead make them give you specific promises. Talk to your friends and family about this issue and if they don't give a fuck out of the goodness in their hearts than guilt them into it by mercilessly assaulting their character. Bully them into faking compassion. Sometimes doing the right thing means being a total bastard. Have no fear in the face of the opposition—let the thought of the boy who might or might not wind up a slave steel your convictions and straighten your middle finger.

Fight for him. Fight for yourself. Fight for a better world. Fight one person at a time.

Spread the word. Kick some ass.

The Mandatory Murder Machine

"It is sad to think that the first few people on earth needed no books, movies, games or music to inspire cold-blooded murder. The day that Cain bashed his brother Abel's brains in, the only motivation he needed was his own human disposition to violence. Whether you interpret the Bible as literature or as the final word of whatever God may be, Christianity has given us an image of death and sexuality that we have based our culture around." – Marilyn Manson, 1999

In 1607 the colony of Jamestown was founded by England. The Algonquins, a Native American tribe rightly pissed at the white man's encroachment into their territory, tried to drive the settlers away. The white men massacred most of them. So begins the history of America.

The white man spread, like a plague, across the American landscape. What he didn't kill, he enslaved. What he didn't enslave, he bound in indentured servitude or wage labor. The natives were systematically all but destroyed, as many as twenty-million slaves were imported to America to work in conditions beyond heinous, the poor Chinamen duped into leaving their homeland to come to America found a society that treated them like dogs on gunned them down the moment they misbehaved.

In 1861, the Civil War began and America was at war with itself. The conflict cost over 600,000 lives—a number beyond our comprehension in this era of modern warfare.

With the end of the Civil War came then end of slavery[41]. Southerners, bitter at their defeat, passed segregation laws, formed racist organizations like the Ku Klux Klan, lynched black men, convicted them of crimes they had not committed and wrought numerous other well-catalogued offenses against them.

I don't have to give you a full history lesson. If you're the least bit attentive, you are well aware of most of our all-American atrocities. Whether we're gunning down out own soldiers like we did in the Bonus March on Washington DC [42] or shooting unarmed protestors as we did in the Kent State shootings[43], we are always working towards the furtherance of our mighty military power-structure.

America is a mandatory murder machine, because it is a machine that runs on blood, and by continuing to live our lives here, we are complicit in every murder America commits to stay afloat.

This is not a new thought by any stretch. You can hear this sentiment from sea to shiny sea, from right- and left-wingers alike.

What may be a new thought, or at least not such an old and over-explored thought, is the notion that it is our morality which has brought about this bloodshed, and only that which we conceive of as immorality can throw a monkey wrench into the spokes of the mighty mandatory murder machine of America. This is, in fact, the entire premise of the book that you hold in

---

[41] Sorta.
[42] http://en.wikipedia.org/wiki/Bonus_march
[43] http://en.wikipedia.org/wiki/Kent_State_shootings

your hands. Every chapter up until this point has been an attempt to defeat true evil—the evil of a system that has subjugated you and everyone you have ever met from the time they were born until this very day.

This system does not function on a single level. It functions on all levels—turning all of your wants and needs against you. With the concept of honor, they [44] have found a means of cementing your conformity to their standards. With their twin prongs of sexual promiscuity and sexual repression, they have left you a confused wreck of insecurity looking to fill the whole inside yourself with any product that you can afford. And if you can't afford it, they'll happily make you pay interest on it for the rest of your life.

In **"Whence Cometh Evil?"** you learned that any notions of moral superiority are rooted in delusion. None of us want this to be the case and perhaps some new knowledge will reveal itself in the future which will invalidate the content of the previous sentence. For now, however, we must accept it as truth.

In **"Honor: Another String Tied To The Human Marionette, Nothing More"** you learned that honor is synonymous with obedience and little more than a means of manipulating you with the currency of respect that human beings naturally long for.

In **"Instant Gratification"** I expounded upon the ways

---

[44] They being those on top—those at the top of the corporate and government hierarchies.

in which Instant Gratification might be beneficial. Some may view this as an endorsement of consumer culture, and in a way it is. I believe that human beings making mistakes is a good thing, because only throughout folly can w advance. A perfect race of flawless beings would, I suspect, still be living in caves.

In **"Obey Your Master"** I examine the American drive to define success only in monetary terms, exploiting the outright vilification of those who dare to define it on any terms but those. In a society with this attitude, gangs of roving drug dealers armed to the teeth should be a surprise to no one.

"Honor Thyself" is about learning how to survive as an individual in a culture that will stop at nothing to destroy individuality. We must be aware of this culture's tricks if we don't want to become just another gear in their machine.

"My Various Failed Subversive Revolutions" was a self-mocking look at my half-baked attempts at disrupting the social norm. It probably has no place in this book, but I thought it too humorous not to include.

"Democracy Is Fascism By Consensus" dispels, with little effort, the notion that the people as an amorphous body should have any say in their governance. The system must exist to protect the individual from the masses, not to protect the masses from the individual. Currently, our system does neither-- both the individual and the masses work in service of the corporations and the government.

In **"Commercials For Mediocrity"** I take a quick

snapshot of the state of television advertisements in America. Nothing gives you a clearer idea of a civilizations values than their ads. Ads appeal to what people really want in life.

In **"Our Heroes"** I point out our tendency to make idiots into heroes, athletes in particular. And why not? They're rich for nothing more than being skilled at the right thing. The world's greatest brick-layer makes 10 bucks an hour, maybe 30 if he's in a union--the world's greatest ball-thrower makes 30 million.

In **"Sorrow & Flatulence"** a chapter that I tried to keep as light-hearted as I possibly could, I relive the death of my father and pass on the lessons of that day to you. I don't know how useful it is to anyone but myself, but the story begged for a place in this book and sometimes you've got to let the words have their way.

"Bitches Be Crazy" is another section that has more of a personal than a political touch, but in America sex and politics are in more dire need of separation than church and state. It would take a whole other book to fully delve into that issue though.

In **"Free and Dumb"** I further build the case that the government views you as property with no more right to control your destiny than a hammer. That's what you are to them--a tool, something to be utilized.

"What Is Freedom?" might sound like a philosophical question, but I examine it in terms that are—at least by my estimation—pragmatic. Ultimately, the chapter must seek to define truth in order to define freedom. They are two concepts that, while not as synonymous as "obedience" and "honor" are inseparable. One cannot be free when one does not have the freedom to pursue the truth.

"The New Slaves" is a strong criticism of the American prison system, which is nothing more than a national string of labor camps where men and women are brutally mistreated and forced into labor against their will for the benefit of corporate America.

And that pretty much wraps things up. Consider the aphorisms in the chapter to follow the closing credits to the cinematic experience that is, "In Defense of Evil" and the two following chapters one of those cool after credit bonuses.

I hope you enjoyed reading it as much as I enjoyed writing it.

50 Aphorisms (In The Nietzschean Tradition)

NOTE: *several of the aphorisms in this section appeared previously in my first book,* **'SCUMBAG: Musings of a Subhuman.'** *They are included here because they are the only part of that book that I am still proud of.*

LOVE AND HATE—It's easy to hate. It's fun to hate. It's comforting, like the buzz from a few pints of ale. It courses through your veins, throbbing, reassuring you or your superiority. When you hate a man, it's easy to watch him die. When you hate a cause, it's funny to see that cause fail. When you hate yourself—truly despise your every breath—there's nothing that can stand in your way.

It's hard to love. It's miserable to be in love or to love a thing. It's stifling, like smoke in the air. It courses through your veins, making you feel small and useless. When you love a person, it's easy for them to stab you in the back. When you love a cause, it's easy for that cause to consume you. When you love yourself—truly adore your every breath—you have everything to lose.

SELF-DECEPTION FOR THE SAKE OF HAPPINESS—Religious people often place personal happiness above the drive towards empirical or personal truth. They will sacrifice any fact or any insight garnered through introspection upon the altar of happiness. They don't want to believe in death because it is too distressing. They don't want to face a cold and unsympathetic universe because it is frightening.

I resent them for the notion that deluding ourselves into believing a falsehood might improve the quality of our existence. It would be absurd for a man with a miniscule penis to live under the impression that it was large and in demand. It would make him feel better, but it would be demonstrably false and would cause him to exist within a world wherein his conclusions about himself were at odds with the conclusions of all others.

Perception is, to some extent, reality—but when perception wholly contradicts the observable to such a degree that others are encumbered by said perception then it becomes the prerogative of the encumbered to instruct the perceiver and guide them, gently if possible, towards the truth.

BEAUTY— I've never seen anything breath-taking. I've never had a moment in my life where my breath was stopped by the sheer perfection of a sight. I've known the intensity of fear, of hate, of self-loathing—but never beauty.

Everything that's supposed to be lovely is offset by the ugliness of my heart. How could I, who lies and hurts at every juncture, look at the beauty of a sunset and feel anything but wretched? The light of beauty only serves to illuminate my emptiness.

    I would like to watch a city burn to the ground from a nearby hillside, huge flames reaching from the buildings to the sky, blotting out the stars with their smoke. That would take my breath away. That would make me feel alive.

    What does that say about me?

PERFECTION—Being perfect is just another imperfection.

GREAT MEN—More great men have died than have ever lived.

ABSOLUTE FREEDOM—In a world of absolute freedom, you own yourself. What you own, you can sell. Therefore, you can sell yourself; you can become another person's property. But then, what if you change your mind? Can you tell them that they no longer own you and leave? If you can, then what did they buy? If you can't, then even absolute freedom isn't absolute.

TRUTH—If the truth is hurtful to someone you care about and a lie is pleasant (and if it is your desire to please them and not to hurt them) then you should be true to your desires and lie to them. It is the most honest course of action.

DECEPTION—The contrary nature of humanity renders the masses more easily deceived by an outright lie than a half-truth.

MISANTHROPY—Misanthropes are the truest humanists. Anyone with love for the human race will find themselves so daily filled with bitterness and disappointment that hatred will become their only means of expressing their love.

RESORT TO VIOLENCE—Why do people always talk about having to "resort to violence." People like violence. They don't resort to it. If anything, people resort to discussion/compromise.

GREATNESS—Humanity is the antithesis of greatness. Only when we cease to be human will we begin to be great.

GREATNESS 2—Who is it that says that not all men can be great? Surely all men can be great in some respect. Otherwise, why should they exist at all?

FEASIBLE GOODNESS—Don't confuse what's feasible with what's just. Don't confuse what's possible with what's good.

THE STRANGER—In this age of constant distraction, we find ourselves very uncomfortable in the moments where we are alone and undistracted. To be alone in this times is the be trapped in a room with a stranger.

SMALL-MINDED GREED—Greed is not a vice. Short-sightedness is. So often, the want for a few trinkets in the immediate costs us the cooperation that could have yielded all of us riches beyond measure.

ACHIEVING POWER—A gang of unremarkable thugs will prevail over the most remarkable of men without fail. Individuals cannot achieve power by opposing the masses, only by controlling them.

THE CRUX OF POWER—The more leashes your hold, the wider and weaker your grip will become.

THE FALLACY FALLACY—When you remove all fallacies from an argument, you wind up with nothing more than disagreement for the sake of disagreement—which is the truth behind all of our disputes, but it's a boring truth so it can go fuck itself.

ALL TRAGEDY IS CONTRAST—Something is alive, then it is dead. Flesh is intact, then it is not. A building stands, then it does not. These are tragedies.

A man dies slowly of a terminal illness. Skin cells die off over time. A building becomes dilapidated and is eventually condemned. These are (though possibly sad) not tragedies.

Why not?

PRINCIPLES—The good thing about being a man of few

principles is that I follow the ones I do have.

SEX OFFENDERS—Only in a country where sex is offensive would we have such a concept as sex offenders. Talking to people on the street you would imagine that sex offenders must be worse by far than any other criminals. The truth is that they are just horny people who did something stupid either because they are sociopathic or because they are too dumb to know better. Having a sex drive doesn't make you a monster, nor does acting upon the sex drive even in defiance of the law. Treating people as though they deserve the worst fate imaginable simply because they engaged in a sex act without the government's seal of approval, however, does make you a monster. More precisely, it makes you part of a monster. You are another cog in the machine whose purpose is the annihilation of liberty.

RAPE-VICTIMS—Rape victims allow themselves to be raped over and over again when they accept special allowances because of their "trauma." For every girl that is raped and milks it for all its worth, ten girls get over it and keep living their lives. The ten need to beat the shit out of the one. She is making it harder for all of them.

DRUNK DRIVING—If old people are allowed to drive then drunks should be too. If they drive recklessly while intoxicated, then arrest them for reckless driving. Otherwise, leave them be.

FUCK AUTHORITY—the reason people cheat so much is because society is so inherently dishonest and inconsistent in what it will and will not allow or tolerate. If people don't respect authority, it's because authority has shown itself to be beneath respect.

GOODY-GOODIES—Anyone who follows the rules just because they're the rules lacks character and intelligence. All intelligent people recognize rules as wholly arbitrary.

HEAD—Blowjobs are the most overrated sexual maneuver of all time. Mouths have teeth in them. Is no one else aware of this? I call the borejobs.

I believe that the only reason most men truly desire blowjobs is because they know that a good number of women still don't like giving them. Men always secretly desire that sex be totally joyless for his partner.

Girls, if you find a man who prefers eating you out to getting a blowjob, then you should fall in love with him regardless of how inadequate he is in all other areas. A man who gives good head is a man dedicated to pleasing you and what he is bad at at first he will improve upon over time.

FANTASY IS BETTER THAN REALITY—This sentiment is only held by people whose dreams have never come true. It's a bitter means of consoling themselves for their boring lives. Reality is better than fantasy because it's real. Even if it falls short of expectation, it surpasses the banality of merely wishing something were happening.

SLEEP DEPRIVATION—I'm a point on a grid. And everything in front of me is expanding to terrifying horizons. The wall in front of me is an infinite distance away. If I got up right now and ran towards it, I would never catch it.

HORROR—The most profound terror doesn't come from what is possible or inevitable, but from the impossible which has somehow been made to seem inevitable.

DENIERS—There is something horrifically wrong with people who deny obvious truths: Evolution, Global Warming, The Holocaust. People who can't stand the truth and have to live a lie are the most pathetic of people, made all the more pathetic by their attempts at building evidence to show how established fact is falsehood.

ANDROGYNY—I read a report that testosterone levels had been steadily decreasing in boys from generation to generation. At the time, as a hairy male who likes violence, I was distraught. Upon further reflection, perhaps a new idea of what is masculine and feminine are called for. The sexes will never be the same, but

I think that all of humanity might benefit from them meeting in the middle.

COMEDY—The greatest comedy is that which is derived from the obsessive compulsive and hyper-judgmental voice inside of all of us. We are all irritants that make each other's lives miserable from time to time. The only ointment that you can apply to misanthropic irritation is humor.

PETTINESS—There is nothing in life so satisfying as doing something completely petty and spiteful to someone whom you revile.

ENEMIES—If your enemy wants to be loved, hate them. If your enemy wants to be hated, be aloof towards them.

ENEMIES 2—Make friends of your old enemies whenever possible and tolerable to keep them from teaming up with your new ones.

LYING—To not tell a lie that you want to tell is to lie to yourself.

BLUNT PEOPLE—People who don't know the truth often speak bluntly in order to conceal this fact.

MUSIC—Many people without souls will claim that they are moved by all kinds music. It is as if they use their love for all music as a means of faking the presence of soulfulness. No soulful person likes all kinds of music. Soulful people like particular sorts of music and despise the rest.

JAILBAIT—It wouldn't be called bait if it weren't tempting.

RELIGION—Religion's greatest crime against man has not been enslavement or war, but stagnation. Without religion, the acceptance of gays is a no-brainer. Without religion the funding of stem-cell research is obviously the correct path. Human society could have advanced tremendously if not for the interference of religion.

CRUELTY—Good cruelty requires imagination. Kindness only requires effort. In other words, one is a skill and the other is merely a chore.

BREAKING THE LAW—The only means of fighting unjust laws is to break them. To stop smoking marijuana in order to legalize its use is like owning slaves while fighting for the cause of abolitionism. If you have deemed a behavior to not be immoral and you have a natural desire to engage in that behavior, then you must do so.

BOOKS—Those who find themselves unsettled and unable to

adjust to daily life are typically those who shun reading. Only through constant reading can we being to appreciate life. Those who don't read are the walking dead.

SMALL PENISES—There is no greater motivator than a small penis. The only cure for which is large sums of money.

TOUCH—Fear of teach is fear of self. Those who put up a barrier between themselves and other are either afraid of being contaminated or afraid of contaminating others. If you know one of these people, touch them relentlessly. If you are one of these people, force yourself to touch others more often.

HOLIDAYS—It is important that some days be special, either anticipated or dreaded. Without these landmarks the calendar would be a bleak place indeed.

MONEY—Only through money and the right attitude towards money can man achieve happiness.

THE RIGHT ATTITUDE TOWARDS MONEY—Money is without value. Possessing mountains of money means nothing, in and of itself. Money is important because with it you can provide a good and lavish life not only for yourself but for those who you care about.

HURTING OTHERS—Never hurt those who have not in some manner invited your wrath. The man who avoids conflict should be left alone, but the man who insults you has invited back any measure of retaliation if he does not heed your warnings to this effect.

ACCEPTING THE IMPERMANENCE OF THINGS—Nothing lasts forever, not even self. You could, as the Buddhist cowards do, detach yourself from all things and renounce your place in this world, but it is far braver and ultimately more gratifying to experience attachment and be strong though periods of separation.

God Of The Godless

"God of the Godless" is a title that I gave myself around the time my subscriber count on YouTube became five figures and people started saying things like, "I can't believe I'm really talking to someone famous!" to me. Most people look at the title as further proof of my massive ego. Very few take the paradox of the distinction to its natural, self-deprecating, conclusion.

God of the Godless is self-negating. It doesn't mean anything. Or, more precisely, it means "nothing." As in, "nothing to see here folks."

The point of the title is that I'm not important. I am an espouser of a particular belief system and it's that belief system that is important. Whether I'm dissecting society's values or making jokes about Skeletor hijacking an airplane, I'm still trying to convey a viewpoint and only you can give that viewpoint any meaning.

Without you there to laugh at my jokes, or nod your head with my grievances, I'm nothing but a fat guy ranting in front of a camera. Only with your support do I become something more than that.

For that, I thank you all.

Eh, who am I kidding, you fuckers are nothing without me! NOTHING! I am spectacularly awesome in every conceivable respect and you're lucky I bother to feign humbleness for even a second! Ha!

Evil Always Triumphs Over Good

The Saturday morning cartoons of my childhood had only one recurring truisms that I remember: "Good always triumphs over evil." Even as a kid I was skeptical of that pronouncement. If a villain murders 200 people and then the hero catches and kills him, then isn't the score 200 to 1 in the villains favor? This notion of good emerging victorious isn't supported by the numbers. Even if the bad guy only killed one person and you kill him for it, good and evil are tied with a score of 1 to 1.

And this is all assuming that it's really good to kill a villain. If he's evil for killing, then why isn't the hero evil for killing? Surely a sentient being is no less sentient and human simply because he has killed others.

Another assumption that I'm uncomfortable with is that everyone who kills people is evil. Was Che Guevara an evil man? I don't agree with his politics or his methods, but I'm not prepared to call him evil because of them.

If there are such things as good and evil than I would say that whatever brings humanity closer to a lasting peace and freedom is good and whatever brings humanity farther from that is evil. Does this make the instruments of these opposing ideologies in and of themselves good or evil? Can any human being be so lacking in complexity that we can stamp them with the good or evil stamp and say, "this is what you are?" No. Only those of foolishly overbearing self-righteousness—the wearers of obscenely shiny good-guy badges would declare a man evil. To believe yourself to be good or evil would require a level of self-deception that I will never be able to muster.

I'm just a man, and though I fight for what I think it good and just with all my might, I will never be able to call myself good. The desire to do evil will never leave me. There's always a bit of Yang in Yin and a bit of Yin in Yang.

I don't speak of balance. It's nothing so orderly and easy to comprehend as that. What I'm talking about, ladies and gentlemen, is grime. There is a thick and potent residue of good on the surface of evil and vice-versa.

Or maybe that's not the truth either. Maybe at the end of the day, it's enlightenment and acceptance of the truth that makes men good and it's ignorance and unfairness and thoughtless cruelty that make men evil.

I hope that this is not the case, because if it is then the majority of the species are evil, and they will always call their evil good and call that which is truly good evil.

If we truly live in that world, a world where the good people—those who hearts are brimming with compassing and soaring heights of understanding and sorrow—are labeled evil by those who are blind to their own evil, then the good will need a defender. Not just one defender, but many—even if their words and deeds for the sake of good will be perceived as **in defense of evil.**

Terroja Kincaid
December 8th, 2008

NECKBEARD UPRISING

T.J. KIRK

I dedicate this book to my loving wife and the undisputed owner of my mind, body and soul, Holly Kirk.

WHO AM I?

1. "GUESS WHO?"

No matter how much I work to dissuade people from being interested in my personal life, many still ask me about it. My aversion to the topic has nothing to do with deep, hidden secrets that I must work to protect. Nor does my reluctance stem from embarrassment or an inability to communicate certain things. I have nothing to hide.

The primary reason that I avoid the topic of my personal life is because I'm actually quite boring. I don't go to parties or social gatherings. I don't hang out with cool people or have interesting adventures. I have no good stories and I have few amusing anecdotes. My autobiography is more the stuff of pamphlets than of memoirs.

Typically, I wake up at around noon, but stay in bed until about one o'clock in the afternoon, lazily contemplating the banalities of life. My wife and I argue over who will take the dog out (I normally lose this argument). I don't shower every day, because it dries out my skin. I shower every other day, spending most of the time making sure that my butt and crotch are not producing odors powerful enough to make birds fall out of the sky.

My wife and I argue over something stupid like which one of us is a "poopface" or a "butthole."

I go downstairs to work on one of my projects—YouTube videos, my website or maintaining my presence on various social networks (Tumblr, Facebook, Twitter). I work diligently to make sure that my fans know that I care about them and that I am eager to produce content for them to the best of my ability.

While I'm doing this, Holly works on keeping the house in order: doing dishes, washing clothes, making dinner. I help her as much as I can and she helps me as much as she can. Because what is marriage for if not to have someone to help you out with your life? Some would say that it's all about forming a strong bond to have and raise children—but Holly and I have little interest in making a child the center of our worlds. We have our own interests and values and children don't yet fit into the world we have made, and are continuing to make, for ourselves.

In the bedroom we snuggle, we talk, we fuck, we watch nature documentaries or Disney movies (Holly is very fond of the repetitious watching of animated Disney films and I've found myself surprisingly amenable to this obsession). If we have weed, we smoke it. If we have no weed, we smoke Black and Milds. She likes to pluck my eyebrows. I like to tickle her thighs. It's not an exciting daily life, but I am content. I've never been one for excitement, if I'm honest with myself.

We tell each other that we love each other constantly, even though we've been together for four years. I think it's because we don't know what else to say sometimes. We both feel so lucky to have the kind of relationship that we have. Sometimes words just aren't enough to express that kind of affection—so we just lay around, holding each other. We're both very affectionate people. We need to smother one another in adoration.

We also both have tempers. So there are times when things are less idyllic, but as we've gotten used to each other, screaming matches have become rare. I think that the fact that I have such a perfect home life is part of the reason I can face down the world with such fearlessness. Without Holly, I have no real center.

2. FIGHTER

Most of the adventures of my life are internal. For instance, I always get a giddy little thrill out of doing something that is (I believe) unethical, yet still socially acceptable, such as eating veal. I love the fact that I'm eating something that never got a chance to live its life at all. Something that my fellow man butchered in its infancy. It feels wrong, and I like that. I like to debase myself by feeling like an evil scumfuck exploiting the moral sluggishness of my own species.

As boring as I am now, I used to be even more so. I never showed emotion. I kept everything inside. I was tranquil and reserved (read:boring) on the surface, even though I was a torrent of extremes within. My emotions were a dull but deep thrum inside of me, hidden behind an impenetrable outer shell of aloofness. This is a sorry state of being, and I have worked, over the years, to rectify it.

The catch-22 of my rehumanization has been that as I have connected with my emotions and learned to express myself, my rage has come to the forefront, and I have found it difficult to constructively cope with. Every single day, it courses through my body like red electric hellfire—compromising my control, affecting my judgment, and eroding my rationality. This came to the fore on a recent trip to Universal Studios in Orlando, Florida.

I was vacationing with my wife, Holly, my brother, Scotty, and his girlfriend, Monica. The plan was to do three days and Disney World and then two days at Universal Studios. Disney World advertises itself as the most wonderful place on earth, but it's oddly comparable to a fascist country. It even has its own secret police.

We started late on our second day at Universal, leaving the hotel at 11:30am and eating a tasty lunch at *Bubba Gump's* in the Universal Citiwalk before making our way to the park. We decided to hit up some shops to buy Monica a pair of sandals. In front of the first store we went to, there was a small crowd of very trashy, rude-looking Cuban people blocking the entrance. Scotty said, "Excuse me." but they didn't move. Scotty isn't the kind of person to repeat himself, so when they failed to move he simply decided to go around them. In the process, he lightly brushed the shoulder of the group's leader—a wannabe 'gangsta' in a blue sports jersey. I don't know what his name was, so I will refer to him hereafter affectionlessly as Douchey.

Douchey was immediately incensed that someone would dare brush against him and began to accost my brother. "Don't touch me bro. You don't need to be touchin' me!"

I turned to Douchey and said, "Do you have a problem?"

Douchey looked at me with the inept rage of a Neanderthal and said something. I don't remember what he said. I just know that the tone seemed threatening, so I pushed him. He flew back—no surprise: I'm big and he was small. He actually hit and knocked down a stroller on his way to the ground and I was scared for a moment that there was a baby inside (I was honestly less concerned for the baby's safety and more concerned with what the consequences would be for me if I contributed to the harming of some random bystanders brat)--but thankfully the stroller was empty. Douchey, shocked from being pushed, got up and got back in my face, "WANNA PUSH ME AGAIN, NIGGA!? YOU A BITCH! YOU A BITCH!"

At this point, I too was filled with Neanderthal rage, but Holly, Scotty and Monica were all working to calm me and assure me that an altercation wasn't in my best interest. Their arguments seemed cogent, and so I relented and turned my back on Douchey. Holly said to him, "This is Universal. Just enjoy your day. Stop being an asshole." Douchey seemed not to hear her. He simply continued to posture as if he were some sort of badass, and my group decided to just go into the store and put the incident behind us.

I knew in my gut, however, that it wasn't over. I knew that Douchey was too embarrassed by our previous encounter to let sleeping dogs lie. I knew that at any moment he would return and attempt to exact his revenge. And sure enough, he did. Barely two minutes had passed before I saw Douchey barge into the store, full of piss and vinegar, looking for a fight.

Security had already arrived at this point and a large, black mountain of a man wearing a security badge blocked Douchey's path to me, but Douchey exploited the layout of the store to find a way around the gigantic security person. Douchey stopped inches from me and proclaimed loud enough for all to hear, "YOU WANNA PUSH ME AGAIN, BITCH?"

"Yes," I said. And I punched him right in his stupid fucking face. The thrill of impact was invigorating—better than anything I've experienced before or since. He reeled back into a shelf, swinging wildly and to no avail. I was calm. I systematically began to work his body. I am not a trained fighter and I'm sure that if I had been, his injuries would have been more severe.

Suddenly, I felt a tremendous force pull me backwards. It wasn't security, as I thought, but Holly. She had used all of her body weight to fling me off of Douchey, losing her own balance in the process. I fell backwards with her and Douchey used the opportunity to kick me several times in the head and ribs—but his kicks were too weak to do any harm.

Unfortunately, after security finally grabbed and subdued Douchey, I found myself quite unable to stand. I couldn't stand at all for a week afterward. Nor could I walk very well for months after that. Today, my leg is much better, but still not 100% of what it was before the fight. And really, it's Holly's fault. It wasn't any of Douchey's attacks that felled me, but Holly's attempt to break the fight up. To this day, I have never been to the doctor for my leg injury. I suspect that I tore my ACL.

I had to fill out an incident report both with the security for Universal's Citiwalk and with the Orlando Police Department. Douchey was ultimately banned from the park for a year. I, on the other hand, was kicked out for the day, but told that I was welcome to return anytime that I liked. Both park security and the employees of the store backed me up on the fact that Douchey was the aggressor, even though I threw the first punch. They wanted to see him get punched in the face every bit as much as I wanted to punch him, and they were joyously happy when I did so. Several employees and store patrons came up to me after the fight as I was sitting on a store bench filling out an incident report, and told me that I was awesome and that me beating the shit out of Douchey was among one of the best things they'd ever seen. I must confess, it's among the best things I've ever done. Or it would have been, if it hadn't come at the high price of my left leg's stability.

It seems that there are few moments of triumph in life that don't come with a price.

But I really don't know how to contain my anger without containing everything else. I don't know how to express all of my emotions *except* for anger. It's all or nothing with me. I am either a cold, distant person who seems to have no emotion. Or I am a cauldron of impotent rage with no focus. My rage is unending. Even now, it is there. I can feel it. A monster beneath my skin. Hating. Screaming. Throwing a tantrum. Demanding that I smash things. Demanding that I punch people in the face. Demanding that I put myself in bad situations. Demanding that I make the bad situations I'm already in worse.

I have no idea how to placate my rage. So it broils and boils and gnarls within my chest, constricting my lungs and overworking my heart. It will not bargain with me. It will not relent.

It will not back down from anyone. Not even me. Especially not me.

My father was an angry man. And it is, I'm almost certain, part of what killed him. My brother is an angry man, and I've seen how it affects him. I've seen how powerless he can become against it. And I know that I am just as powerless against my own anger.

Of course, it can be fun to be angry. More often, however, it's a tremendous liability. I no longer feel glee when I verbally eviscerate someone. I no longer get a burst of joy from smashing something. I no longer want my daydreams of going on a rampage. I want this fire tamed. Not put out. But tamed. I want to control my anger. Right now, it controls me. I am not the master of my hatred. It is my master. And when, on a cold day, my left leg aches and tightens up, I am reminded of the toll I have already paid for allowing my rage to hold the reigns.

At the same time, it's hard to deny that rage has been good to me. I am an extremely belligerent and contentious asshole, and people seem to like that. If anything, people wish I was more belligerent. The more contentious I become, it seems, the more views I get on YouTube. It seems that no one wants to "like" me in any sort of traditional way. People want to be entertained by me, by my ranting and raving and screaming and yelling.

Be honest. Who would you rather watch in a debate? Two kindly folks having a civil disagreement or two bitter enemies who hate one another and view each other as lower than dog shit?

If you answered the former you are either part of a very tiny minority or you are a fucking liar. People love to see two assholes go head to head. Do you think my YouTube inbox every week is stuffed to the brim with people asking me to nicely refute idiots on YouTube? No. It's full of requests for me to cruelly obliterate idiots with extreme prejudice and zero empathy. So, from an entertainment standpoint, there is at least one pro to being an emotionally stunted rage-o-holic. It's more entertaining, and if you're not entertaining then who is going to watch? Who is going to listen?

But that does bring up a big follow-up question, doesn't it? Why am I worth listening to? What about me makes me uniquely qualified to speak up and to speak out? I'm a reasonably intelligent man, but there are smarter ones. I can speak eloquently, but many have oratory gifts that put mine to shame. I am not an expert on any subject, nor am I a strong advocate of or activist for any particular position.

That's a hard question for me to answer, because I have such a low opinion of myself. My depression, though held at bay by sheer force of will, still whispers to me: *"27 years old? You're nearly 30. What the fuck have you accomplished? You fat fuck. You'll never lose weight. You're fucking ugly. You suck at life. You fail. No one likes you. No one cares about you. Every relationship you have is a fucking lie. Either you're lying to them or they're lying to you. You're rotten to the core. Why would anyone love someone like you? You are a shit smear on the face of the world, and the napkin is coming. You're going to be wiped away. The word pathetic is too generous an adjective to apply to you. You are beneath contempt and beyond insignificance. You mean nothing. You have no positive traits. Everything about you is coarse and grating and undesirable. If you were in a movie, you would be the scumbag janitor who spends too much of his time staring at High School girls. If you were a lawyer, you'd be a personal injury lawyer who went to night school. If you were a banker, you'd be one of the ones in prison for embezzling. If you were a McDonalds french fry, you'd be one of the soggy brown ones that no one wants."*

The thing that people who don't suffer from depression may not understand is that depression is more than just sadness. Sadness is something that everyone faces in life. Sadness is an aspect of depression, but far from the totality of depression.

Depression makes it difficult to feel positively about future prospects. Depression makes it difficult to emotionally invest in present endeavors, even things that once held your interest. Depression makes you miserably lonely but makes you feel unable/unwilling to seek out human contact.

Nothing feels right when you're depressed. Everything feels like it doesn't matter and yet matters more than anything. You feel too depressed to do things and then you feel depressed about the things you didn't do. It's vicious. It's cyclic. It's unrelenting. It goes much deeper than mere pessimism or sadness. It's a form of psychological paralysis.

You feel crippled inside. And no one else can see it. No one sees the invisible barrier that prevents you from being who you want to be. Even these words truly fail to capture how it feels. Only those who have experienced it or are currently experiencing it will truly understand.

My advice to my fellow sufferers is this: break the cycle. The worst thing about depression is that it forces us to feel powerless to escape the self-fulfilling prophecy of our own unhappiness. You have to make a conscious effort to prove depression wrong. When it says that you don't have confidence, you have to defy it. You have to say, "Fuck you, Depression. I can do this." Even if you don't really believe it, you have to conduct yourself as if you do.

Soon enough, Depression will lose its grip over you. Don't get me wrong, you'll still be depressed, but you'll have learned to work around it.

And don't believe anyone who tells you that you are powerless. Find your passion. Only passion can defeat depression. I'm sure that part of the reason why I am so quick to anger is because I have to wear that rage on my sleeve. Otherwise the ennui will begin to dig its tendrils in, sucking out life, pumping in lethargy. Fuck that. You have power. Depression is a chemical imbalance? Well, guess what? All of your thoughts are chemical. You can think your way out of depression. Don't get me wrong. It never goes away. Your battle will never be over. But you can confine the beast to some small corner of your mind and spit in its face when it tries to sing you back into a somnolent stupor.

In other words, you learn to live with the imbalance. A man who is missing a leg can't will his leg to grow back, but he can teach himself to live with one leg. That's what you must do with depression. When you feel as if you simply cannot act, you must act anyway. You must say to your inner sense of dread, "FUCK YOU. I WILL DO THIS."

Chemical imbalance really is a shaky excuse for

being psychologically crippled. Balance is a human notion. We're the ones who like to think that things need to be balanced or in a certain proportion, but that's just an illusion. The reality is that things are free to vary, free to take on shapes, sizes and natures wildly different from what we expect or view as proper or correct.

My opinion has always been that if you don't like the chemistry of your brain, alter it. We have a plethora of technologies and techniques available to fiddle with brain chemistry. Those content to bitch about how bad they feel are cowards, because they refuse to attempt to change their own shitty situations. When I was depressed—and I was for years—I looked for ways to solve the problem.

Now, as people become more weak-willed and wishy-washy, they denounce people who take my approach to dealing with depression. I've tried to council a lot of people who end up telling me that I'm not accepting of their illness. Accepting of their illness? Are these people fucking idiots? We don't accept illness. We fight it. Or we die.

Everyone has obstacles in life. Some come from within, others are external. Some people have anger issues, others have radical mood swings, obsessive-compulsions, split personalities, paranoid delusions, massive insecurities, social anxieties, crippling phobias and dozens of other mental obstacles that they must deal with. Other people have physical disabilities, unwanted dependents, crazy spouses, serious financial problems, medical bills, ruthless enemies, problems at work, etc. Depression is just one of many problems in the human condition.

That's what I say to depressed people. Fight or die. Or at least stop your moaning. I've grown weary of the bleating of cowards, and with seven billion fuckers on this planet, it's not like the lives of these people are so precious that we can't afford to lose them. Don't get me wrong, I'd much prefer that they overcome their depression and be happy, but if they won't even try then I don't see why I should sympathize with them. Especially when I've done that which they claim is impossible.

Ultimately, dealing with rage, depression and social anxiety my entire life has given me a very different view of life and the human condition than most people. Most people start off idealistic and become cynical over time. I started off cynical and I'm trying—desperately—to find something to be idealistic about. I'm trying to find something about my species that gives me hope. Thus far, I've come up short. I've failed to find humankind's great redeeming characteristic. Have I failed to find it because it's not there or because of some flaw in my own internal processes? We'll explore that more in the next chapter.

Is that what makes me worth listening to? The fact that I never fell in with any clique? That I never belonged anywhere? That I never drank anyone's Kool Aid?

I don't know if anyone out there is stupid or crazy enough to consider me to be a source of wisdom, but if even one such person exists, I have to share with them the most important thing I know. Perhaps it is something that most people already know, and that I am only just now finding out.

I've never been like most people. In some ways, I'm proud of that, but mostly I just feel like everyone is speaking a language that I don't understand. Then again, maybe everyone feels that way. Maybe there are as many different languages as there are different people. But that's not my wisdom. That's just an observation that will probably be labeled pretentious by people who use words like pretentious to hide the fact that they lack any real criticisms.

My wisdom is this: the people who hate you will hate you no matter what concessions you attempt to make. They will hate you if you repent. They will hate you if you clarify. They will hate you if you attempt to explain. Don't attempt to reason with people that hate you. They don't want to understand you, they only want to defeat you. To them, life is a contest to see who can be the most right or perceived as the most moral. Things like understanding and finding a middle ground are beyond them. They're not worth your time or your effort.

There is a quote, by Friedrich Wilhelm Nietzsche. He said: "He who fights with monsters might take care lest he thereby become a monster. And if you gaze for long into an abyss, the abyss gazes also into you." It's long been my favorite quote, but I've failed to heed it's warning. I have, in fact, dedicated my life to fighting monsters and staring into the abyss. And I don't want to do it anymore. But it's all I know how to do.

3. YOUTUBER

I'm just not what anyone pictures when they imagine a popular YouTuber. If you look at the types of people who become big on YouTube, they look like the people who were fucking popular in high school. Wretched people with big smiles and little brains. Small picture people with timidity in their hearts—complete capitulation to conventionality is their credo.

And it's harder than people think to be a YouTuber. I have to monitor news and cultural trends. I have to do everything in my power to make sure that I'm relevant and entertaining. And if I fail, I have nothing. I don't have a safety net to fall back on. It's either I make my audience laugh or I die.

If they don't find me entertaining, I don't have another skill to fall back on. This is it for me. If I'm ever cutthroat, it's because my livelihood is on the line. I fear every day that I will lose this thing that I have built for years. I am terrified that people will simply lose interest and find something better to do with their time.

I don't live in the lap of luxury. I don't have health insurance. I have ratty clothes. I make money, but I spend a lot of it trying to build a website that I hope will be successful enough to give me a little bit more security than I have now. The rest I spend making sure that my family—my wife and my brother—are taken care of. I'm not nominating myself for sainthood here. I'm just trying to make something clear to you: I'm a working man. I don't get endless respect for minimal effort. I work 7 days a week trying to ensure that me and my loved ones have a future.

And in the process I've helped others (people who are like me). And I've made money. But what have I done to myself? I've stunted my growth as a person to keep myself entertaining. I've trained myself to feel constant anger because that's what sells. I've lived so publicly that I can't even have a private thought anymore. Everything is Tumblred, Tweeted, Facebooked or YouTubed. I used to just look at my wall or ceiling and think about life. Now all I do is stare at my phone or my computer, wondering what I should tweet next. What little real thinking I do is geared towards being entertaining. Every idea I have is boiled down to it's most basic essence so that it can be easily digested by a mass audience. I'm the reverse Pinocchio! I went from being a real boy to being a puppet—which truly is counterproductive to the emotional journey that is my life's ultimate goal: find an ideal, and find a reason to care about the world and everyone in it. Find some way to reconnect with your humanity. Shed this aloofness.

How long can I do it? How long can I make videos for you and for all the others? Well, I will continue to do it until I no longer have the fire in my belly to say what I have to say. My passion ebbs and flows, but it's never receded entirely into nothingness. If that happens, I'll stop and find something else to do.

4. HUSBAND

I'd say I was a total failure in that regard if not for my wife, Holly. I have very bad social anxiety, especially when it comes to crowds, but oddly I wasn't nervous in the days leading up to our wedding. We had a small guest list compared to some (about 100 people) but it was still big enough to warrant a small panic attack. Yet, I wasn't nervous. My stomach felt fine. My pulse was normal. I didn't feel stressed.

But about five minutes before I walked down the aisle to take my position, my stomach felt like it shrank to the size of a dime. My lungs stopped working. My heart began throbbing. My legs got so tense they were hard to bend at the knee. I guess my nerves caught up to me.

Galen, a good friend of mine, saw my distress and pulled me aside for a quick pep talk that consisted of this: "No one looks at the men at these things. No one gives a fuck about you. Everyone's looking at the women and their colorful dresses. You're just some piece of shit they don't care about." This calmed me down enough to get me out there. And before long, my shyness melted away through the sheer socializing power of booze.

Holly and I are a good team. I don't really know how to write about our relationship. I feel that it could be a book unto itself if I wanted it to be. I will say that she is the only person who stands by me for all that I am. Everyone else backs away from certain aspects of my personality, no matter how charmed they are by others. She's the only person that accepts every facet of my being. And I accept all of her.

She has trouble being herself around other people. She puts up a front, and most people like that front. But I know the real Holly—and I'm glad I do. She has a great sense of humor, a great sense of play and is very devoted to me and to us. I like the fact that even after four years with me, she is still very attached, still gives me a lot of affection, still accepts a lot of affection from me. I have done a lot of things wrong in my life, but making Holly my life-mate was not one of them. She is, I think, the best decision of my life—the only decision I've ever made that *truly* improved the quality of my existence.

A lot of people seem curious about my marriage, particularly due to my staunch atheism, but I would say that just because I recognize no gods doesn't mean I can't appreciate ceremonies and their real world significance to flesh and blood human beings. Marriage is a ritual. It's an act of consecration that goes beyond the mere "religious." It's a set of regimented behaviors and legal bindings designed to make a declaration to yourself, your friends and family, and above all to your partner, that you dedicate your existence to them.

It's not all about love. Love is just part of it. It's about an alliance of two people. It's the statement that you and your partner vow to put the interests of the couple above the interests of the individual. It says to the world, "We are each other's property, and so we are both owners of a new joint entity, an amalgam of two people, now brought together and made one."

That's how I view it, anyway.

It's funny, because for a long time I let other people convince me that I couldn't love. I'd been told before that I'm not capable of loving someone. That I am like a reptile. Cold. Unfeeling. Dark and unsympathetic. There is truth to some of that, but I am capable of love. Perhaps I am too capable of love. I have a wife, and I love her. I also have another girl, who lives far away, and I love her as well. There's more. Different people—not all girls—whom I have varying levels of affection for and attraction to. I find things I can love in all of them.

What attracts me to a person? Damage? Darkness? Yes, those are factors. No one sane and healthy could ever give me the sort of affection I need or desire. I'm not a simple man. I'm not a normal soul who can content himself with the mechanics of standard human sex acts. Nor can my dreams be talked to sleep by the superficial kinks peddled to the masses. I have needs that rage in me like a volcano that will not go inactive until it bathes the entire world in its molten lava.

But Holly is the undisputed sun in my solar system. She is the center. She is the object with the greatest gravitational force. I revolve around her.

5. SUPER FAMOUS PERSON

Anyone who knows me knows that I hate one place on earth more than any other: and that place is Wal-Mart. I only go there if there's simply no other choice.

One time, I am standing in the Wal-Mart check out line, holding whatever accursed thing I've ventured in to purchase. Part of me (most of me, if I'm honest) wants to just throw the money at the cashier, scream "Keep the change!" and run.

It is at that moment that the strangest looking human being that I've ever seen walks up to me and stands a mere two inches away. He looks up at me (he's short) and says, "Amazing Atheist?" His voice is reedy. His breath stinks. He looks like a vastly uglier version of Steve Buscemi crossbred with a newborn bird.

"Yeah," I say. "That's me."

"Fan," he says, sticking out his gaunt hand for a shake.

To be polite, I take it. It feels cold, like the hand of a corpse.

Then he walks away, leaving me to wonder if he was a real person or a ghostly apparition that chose that moment to fart forth from the ectoplasmic sphincter of hell to confound me with his presence for a moment. He never said more than those three words to me.

Encountering fans isn't always that strange, but it's always at least a little strange. Some people just want to say hi or get a handshake. Others want pictures. No one has ever wanted an autograph before. I have been interrupted mid-meal before, however, by a Christian. Do unto others? Peh. Would he like some stranger interrupting his dinner to debate him? I think not. I was polite to him, but I was not obligated to be by circumstance, since he was being extremely rude to me by disrupting my meal and my conversation with my friends.

There was another guy in a laundromat who shook my hand when he recognized me, but immediately said in a very sour voice that he was not a fan of my work. I shrugged and said I was sorry to hear that. He later wrote about how I must be trailer trash because I was at the laundromat—I guess he forgot that the only reason he knew that was because he was there too.

6. INSOMNIAC

Some strange shit happens when you go for a long time without sleep. Sounds get deeper. And I don't mean deep like Leonard Cohen's voice, I mean deep like the ocean. The sounds feel like they are threatening to encompass you. And they feel farther away.

Another odd thing: my head always feels like it's wherever it *was*, as opposed to wherever it *is*. I feel like my sense of my own head's position is on a three second delay. So, intellectually, I know my head is in position B, but my gut tells me that it's still in position A—even though position A was seconds ago.

This too is strange: everything is boring, even if it's not. When you're sleep-deprived you can be excited, and bored with your excitement at the same time. Bored excitement. Dull fervor.

And strange thoughts!

7. NOISY NEIGHBOR

I used to have a neighbor named Bo who was insane about noise. Now, before you decide that I'm an incredibly loud and inconsiderate person who is just unaware of what a douche bag I am, let me make my case.

The first problem I had with him was when I was watching a Nostalgia Critic video late at night with my friend, Galen. At first, we were watching the video fairly loudly, so I didn't begrudge my neighbor for tapping on his ceiling (he lived below me) to get me to shut up. After I turned it down, his banging continued. So I turned it down even more. To the point where even I could barely hear it over the sound of my my own breath.

My asshole neighbor came upstairs and banged on my door, demanding that I turn the sound off or he would call the police. I told him, "Fuck you. Call the police." And he did! The police showed up. They told me to keep it down. I told them that I was keeping it down, but my neighbor was just a lunatic.

A few months later, my landlord called me and told me to shut my toilet lid more gently, because Bo was complaining that the momentary *clack* of the toilet lid closing was profoundly disturbing to him. I started shutting the lid softer, since it was clear at this point that my landlord was taking my neighbor's side.

Bo also complained if I walked too loudly (or walked at all too late at night.)

Bo tried to physically fight me and call the police on me several more times after that first major incident. Each time for making very little noise. None of my other neighbors ever complained. In fact, I asked my next door neighbor if he had any issues with my noise levels and he told me that he'd never heard a peep.

I was told by my landlord that this man, Bo, had complained about the noise of the traffic outside, the noise of people entering the apartment building late at night, the noise of crickets in the grass out in front of the building, etc. This man was not rational, yet everyone was terrified of confronting him because of his violent temperament.

Finally, I had enough. I moved out of the apartment months before my lease was up. I don't think I will ever be able to live in an apartment again. My life was turned into constant stress by this one man. For months afterward, I couldn't walk on my house's floor without tip-toeing around because I subconsciously thought I might set off the powder keg of a neighbor living below me. And every time I realized that I didn't have to worry about him anymore, it was a tremendous relief.

Perhaps the most ironic thing of all about this

whole situation is that my neighbor would constantly get into screaming matches with his college-aged son. So this noise-hating psycho was, in and of himself, incredibly loud. I would have to listen to him berate his son at the top of his lungs at least once a month.

Even after I moved out, Bo still wound up giving me a little bit more grief. I had rented too small of a Uhaul and so I'd had to make more than one trip to get all my stuff. I didn't arrive at the house to collect my last few things until 3 in the morning. There were only a few things left inside and it only took us 15 minutes to pack all of the remaining stuff—but Bo spent the entire 15 minutes yelling at me and my friends that we weren't supposed to be there and that I was supposed to be out by midnight and I was trespassing. He even called up my Landlord (at 3AM!). I ended up talking to my Landlord on Bo's phone and trying to calm the situation.

I kept telling Bo, "Why do you give a shit? I'm leaving. We won't be neighbors anymore. This is the last you'll ever have to deal with me. Why are you trying to create an altercation?" He was no amenable to this logic. Galen was less geared towards a peaceful resolution and kept taunting Bo, daring him to do something. But of course, Bo didn't do anything. He talked pretty much constantly about kicking people's asses, but he had no real follow-through.

8. ZEN MOTHERFUCKER

When I was 13, I was made fun of for being the boy with breasts. My fat has always liked to deposit itself on my chest, and the bigger I got, the bigger my boy tits got. Well, now they're man tits.

The older I've gotten, the more I've realized that other people are going to give you shit no matter what you do or how you look or what you are. People are just assholes. You just have to keep your chin up and learn how to look them right in the eye and say, "Fuck you. I'm proud to be me." I consider that to be my pursuit of happiness.

Most people who strive for happiness are embroiled in misery. They don't want happiness for some property that happiness holds; they want happiness because to them, it represents an end to their internal torment.

I don't really seek happiness any longer. Nor do I run from pain. I exist, and I seek out that which interests me. I do that which feels worth doing. What emotional reward it will give me is not foremost in my mind.

The odd thing is this: when you let go of your concern for your emotional well-being, you find that, more often than not, you are content. There will be anger and there will be sorrow and there will be boredom—but that's fine. Those are just states of being and they, like happiness, are ephemeral. And it is possible to look at them rationally, even when you are in the throes of them.

I am not a hedonist. I do not hold pleasure above all things. Nor do I seek refuge from my pain. Nor do I ignore my needs for pleasures and my needs for pains. I simply follow my passions, wherever they may lead.

I call this attitude bullshit zen. And it came in handy recently in my pursuit of losing weight. My most valuable advice on weight loss, however, is don't listen to the people who think they're experts. Everyone thinks you've "got" to do this. Or you've "got" to do that.

Fuck them.

You know what you've got to do on a diet? Eat good food. Even if that, to you, is a bunch of cupcakes. Dieting isn't worth being miserable. Food is supposed to give pleasure and life, not be a substance you fear and dread.

When someone sees you eating bacon and says, "Aren't you supposed to be on a diet?" then say back to them, "Aren't you supposed to be minding your own fucking business?"

Trust me. I've actually lost weight. Most people who give diet advice are people who have always been skinny and don't know what the fuck they're talking about.

My diet is that I try to eat less shitty than I want to eat. For instance, I want to eat fried chicken slathered in gravy with a side of mac and cheese and some cake for dessert; wash it all down with a coke.

Maybe I overhaul the whole meal and get grilled chicken, steamed broccoli and water. Not likely though! I'll usually get at least one of the things I actually want. I'll get the grilled chicken, but still do the mac and cheese. Or I'll get the grilled chicken and steamed broccoli but still treat myself to dessert.

The one thing I certainly don't try to do is believe in myself. Believing in yourself is too damn hard. I try, instead, to believe in the science of what a diet is. I can believe that lowering my intake of fats and carbohydrates will make me a thinner person. I can believe that with stretching and exercise, I can make myself healthier and more desirable to many people. I believe all of that, because there are facts behind it. There are verifiable results as I discover that I weigh a little bit less each week.

But I can't believe in myself. I know that I am weak-willed. I know that I am going to feel like I could conquer the world one minute and feel like a worm on a hook the next. I know that I can't rely on my own willpower, because it will falter.

Granted, my bullshit zen is a form of willpower, but it's not derived from total self-reliance. It is instead derived from reliance on the external facts that are true regardless of how I think or feel about them.

9. THE UNBEATABLE

I have strong opinions, and strong opinions create strong backlash. And since I don't take anyone's side completely, everyone feels like I'm against them. I'm not accepted on the left or the right, by the feminists or the MRAs (that's Men's Rights Activists, and yes, they exist), by the active or the apathetic. I'm just the subhuman schmuck who calls everyone on their bullshit, and no one can call me on mine because I preemptively call myself on it.

They can't beat me, because I'm not even playing the same game they are. So, they lash out with as much vitriol as they can, trying to demean me, to tarnish whatever reputation they think I have.

I don't let it bother me on a personal level, but I wish that they would be more open-minded to my perspective for their own sake—because they're making themselves look bad, not me. They've shown that truth means nothing to them. They're hacks wearing their ideological bias on their sleeves.

And perhaps someone could turn that around on me. Perhaps to someone else's view I am a drone too and a hypocrite to boot. Well, so what if I'm hypocritical? I think that puts me on even footing with the other seven billion hypocrites on planet earth. Do you think you're not a hypocrite? Do you honestly believe that your thoughts and feelings conform 100% to some cockamamie notion of rational consistency that you've cooked up?

Not only am I a hypocrite—I am proud of my hypocrisy. I am proud that my passions are powerful enough to overwhelm me and create those interesting instances of cognitive dissonance that are really the things that make a person interesting, complex and vital.

Why should I care if I seem hypocritical or unlikable in the eyes of people who have no comprehension of my words and view everything on a superficial, surface level, never looking at the subtext, never reading between the lines, never doing anything but reacting to their buttons being pushed. I love to mock those who are pitifully predictable, and coerce them into making my points for me—all while lacking awareness that they're being played like a cheap fiddle in the hands of a master musician. Do you think I'm unaware that I often come across as brash and arrogant? Do you imagine that I am incapable of feigning humility the second it suits my agenda?

Am I revealing my true feelings now, or am I leading you deeper into the mire of some grand deception? I am too clumsy to perform sleight of hand, but I can use the principles of magic to misdirect you with one idea while actually espousing another. It's all a game for me.

Or is it?

I suppose I come across as a bit egotistical here. I should probably contextualize it a bit. You see, no one ever thought of me as intelligent when I was growing up. I was always primarily considered weird, and it was a distinction I reveled in and an identity I heartily embraced. I never had to dress weird. My behavior and esoteric interests were enough to brand me indelibly as "that weirdo." At some point, I engaged in strategic propaganda, designed to enhance this reputation. I'd do things like stand up in the middle of class and shout, "I AM A VAMPIRE! YOU ARE ALL BENEATH ME!"

That behavior is ultimately what led to my current personality. I was formed by my environment, to an extent, just as all people are.

10. KNOCK KNOCK

Who's there? Me. I am everything listed above and many, many things that are not even touched upon. Perhaps one day I will devote more time to the subject of who I am and what makes me tick, but my ego isn't yet big enough to sustain such an effort just yet. My megalomania has only advanced enough to sustain a giant rambling chapter devoted to myself—not an entire book.

Not yet, anyway.

PASSIVELY ENTERTAINED BY DRIVEL AND GLITTER

I was asked once what I would do to Justin Bieber and Nicki Minaj if given the chance. After much deliberation, I decided that I'd give Justin and Nicki a 3 foot long double-sided dildo (with a 12 inch circumference). Their lube: hot sauce. One end of the dildo goes in Nicki's ass. The other end goes in Justin's ass. And whoever gets it in farthest gets to die relatively quickly. The loser has to starve to death in a room where their own shitty music is blaring at top volume. It's not sadistic. It's only fair! Let them suffer as I have suffered—as *WE ALL* have suffered. The great thing about this solution, is that it gives Justin and Nicki an opportunity to be genuinely entertaining in their otherwise boring careers.

I am not a tremendous fan of much of the things that the average person finds entertaining. I don't care for pop music, NY Times Bestsellers, crime procedurals or reality shows (though I will own up to Pawn Stars as a guilty pleasure). I think that stupid entertainment creates a stupid populace. Art is supposed to be food for thought, but nearly everything that becomes popular now seems to be the artistic equivalent of Doritos—superficially tasty, but of no nutritional value.

By far, one of the worst examples of our cultural decline, is the popularity of Michael Bay's horrendous Transformers movies. Reprinted below is my review of the third (but unfortunately not final) addition to the series:

I am dead inside. I am dead and my soul is mush and my heart is dust and my brain is missing. I have just seen 'Transformers: Dark Of The Moon.' The only moon worth speaking of in this movie is the dimpled moon of Michael Bay's pale white butt as he squats down, pulls open his asshole, and releases this movie into America's eager, gaping maw, browning our teeth and indelibly tarnishing our spirits.

This cinematic abomination opened tonight in IMAX 3D, and I saw a sold out (fuck you, America) showing at **AMC 20 Palace Place** in Harahan, Louisiana. Because the movie was sold out, we had to show our tickets as we entered the theater. The first time I showed it, the dull-eyed usher said, "It's backwards." The ticket was backwards. I'd been careless. I flipped it around so he could see the front. "It's upside down," he said testily.

Pissed, I flipped it right side up and held it literally a centimeter in front of his face and continued holding it there as he stared blankly forward. No matter what he said in acknowledgment, I continued to hold it there, hoping to incite his ire. I saw the rage and indignation begin to well-up in his stare and I finally removed my ticket from his site and loudly proclaimed him to be a douche bag. He got the last laugh, however, because I was in for Transformers 3.

The movie began with an explanation that the space race of the 1960's was actually because a spaceship had crashed onto the moon and we had to beat the soviets to it. The scenes explaining this are run through so fast that you feel like the movie is being edited by a meth-freak with an attention span measured in micro-seconds. It felt as if Michael Bay were resentful that he had to actually tell a story and wanted to get through it as quickly as possible so that he could get to the movie he really wanted to make: tight shots on Rosie Huntington-Whiteley's ass/tits and gratuitous amounts of often nonsensical explosions.

Why do I say it was "as if" Michael Bay resents story? He does. He simply hates narrative structure and character development. Michael Bay doesn't just breeze through story elements, he blasts through them as quickly as he can like an ADHD child unwrapping Christmas Presents. He shows utter contempt for storytelling as an art form. He views plot, story and character as things that exist to taint his otherwise perfect universe of PG-13 sensuality and wanton violence.

Shia Labitch returns as the repugnant crybaby "hero" of our story, Sam Witwicky. I'm all for complaining, ladies and gentlemen, but this asshole complains about everything, even though his life is amazing. In the first film, he's a white teenager from an upper middle-class family and he whines about his dad being a cheapskate. Fine. He's an adolescent.

In the second film, he's a young adult who's dating Megan Fox, owns a sexy Camero that turns into a giant robot who will do anything to protect him and his parents are footing the bill for him to attend an Ivy League school where even more girls inexplicable want to sleep with him. Sounds pretty sweet, right? Well, he still manages to bitch about it.

In this newest film he has a brand new girlfriend of implausible hotness who has a gorgeous house, a cushy job and supports him both emotionally and financially. AND HE'S STILL A WHINEY FUCKING BITCH! Why? Because he feels that his life isn't meaningful enough. You saved the world twice you fucking asshole! How much more significant do you need your life to be?

Sam literally spends the first 40-60 minutes of the movie complaining about how no one recognizes how awesome he is and boasting to everyone he meets about how he saved the world twice and got a medal from the President. This is what passes for heroism in the 21st century folks: fuck selflessness, fuck humility, fucks reluctance, fuck struggle—it's all about the bragging rights. I saved the world, man, isn't that cool? It's akin to Superman **wishing** for Brainiac to come along and kill some people so that he can save the day and Metropolis can see how cool he is for the 700th time.

Sam's girlfriend, Carly, as played by Rosie Huntington-Whiteley, is hardly even worth mentioning. She has the personality of a box of Nilla Wafers. Sugary and boring. She exists mainly as one of Michael Bay's props. He might as well have stapled a pair of tits and an ass onto a mop for all the liveliness she injects into the role.

I also regret to inform you that Kevin Dunn and Julie White are back as Sam's unwatchably grating parents. I guess they're supposed to be comedy relief, but they only serve to cement your despair—it's like being forced to see Jay Leno monologues in between having your teeth pulled. It's not a relief, comedic or otherwise. It's insult to injury.

The Transformers themselves are interchangeable masses of metal. As far as I can tell, the principle difference between the autobots and the decepticons is that the decipticons tend to have sharp teeth and be more drably colored. I guess there's a philosophical difference between the two of them as well? One is generically good and the other is generically evil. It's never explained beyond that. Freedom and tyranny are tossed around as concepts, but neither is explored in the slightest.

    The plot really doesn't matter much, but it boils down this: there are these things called pillars that look like big metal dildos and they're capable of opening a huge portal. The decepticons have them, but they can only be used by Sentinel Prime, who was the former leader of the autobots. He disappeared shortly before the end of the original war between the autobots and the decepticons and it was his ship, carrying the pillars, that crashed into the moon back in the 60's.

    Here's where it gets dumb (even dumber, I mean). Sentinel Prime betrays the autobots. It turns out that before the destruction of cybertron (the transformers' home planet) Sentinel Prime and Megatron made a deal that Sentinel Prime would meet Megatron on earth and they would transport their entire planet to earth's atmosphere so that humans could be used as slave labor to repair the *planet. So, yeah, Sentinel Prime is evil. I will now list all of the reasons why this is fucking retarded:*

- *In the first film, it was said that Megatron was discovered frozen in ice in 1894. How long he was there, we don't know, but that means this deal couldn't have been made before 1894. In 1894 there were only about 1.5 billion people on earth, with little grasp of technology whatsoever. Megatron and Sentinel Prime conspired together to get 1.5 monkeys (most of whom had yet to industrialize) to rebuild their technologically advanced planet?*
- *Why would they make that deal when the allspark still existed at that time? The allspark had the power to restore cybertron, and Megatron had come to earth to find it according to the first film. So, was this plan with Sentinel just his shitty back-up plan?*
- *If Megatron is the leader of the decepticons and Sentinel Prime was the leader of the autobots, then how could Sentinel Prime be a traitor? When two leaders agree to end a conflict and fight for a common goal, their followers tend to—I don't know—FOLLOW!*

- *I'm sure it probably conflicts with some of the plot points in Revenge of the Fallen as well, but honestly I can't bring myself to even remember what the plot of that movie was at this point.*

None of this matters, however, since the movie drops the plot entirely after the first hour in favor of the longest, most mind-numbingly boring, non-stop "action" sequence I have ever had the misfortune of suffering through. Chicago is destroyed so many times over that you start to swear you've seen the same building fall 10 times by the time it's done. You don't care about anyone on either side and, in the case of the Transformers, you can barely tell them apart. Stuff explodes. Everyone gets dirty but Carly (because I guess Michael Bay doesn't think dirty girls are hot). Her ability to stay clean in a city rocked with explosions, collapses, dust, dirt, fire and ash would be a glaring inconsistency in most movies—here it's almost expected.

At the end of the movie, almost as if Michael Bay ran out of time, Optimus Prime suddenly becomes a super badass and kills all of the decepticons in like 30 seconds. I wanted to scream at the screen, "Why didn't he fucking do that in the first place!?" He could have saved me hours of my time and, more importantly, my sanity.

After the film, my mind was so numb that my family and friends found me wandering the parking lot like a lost dog, unable to speak, unable to process what I'd just suffered. Don't see this movie.

Bay's Transformer films are particularly egregious example of how mind-numbingly awful much of our entertainment is, but he's not unique in his pandering to the lowest common denominator. And when it comes to movies, I think a good deal of the blame for this lie with the lackluster crop of critics that currently populate sites like Rotten Tomatoes.

Kung-Fu Panda 2's positive reviews are a good example of this decline in standards. Kung-Fu Pando 2 is an inept work of brain-dead cinema that substitutes racial stereotypes and bright colors for character development and a coherent narrative. I defy anyone to describe any of the secondary characters to me without relying solely on their appearance. Is the monkey smart? Is the crane tenacious? We don't know. We don't care. They're just there as toy-fodder for Happy Meals so that kids across America can be as fat as the kung-fu panda themselves.

I'm told I'm a cynic for hating movies like this, but the real cynics are the jaded assholes who peddle this pablum to us and expect us to accept it. And we reward their cynicism with rave reviews and financial success! No one made Kung-Fu Panda 2 because it was a story that burned in their chest, a story that they just had to share with the world. It was made for the sole purpose of making fat wads of greasy money by pandering to the dumb masses—a fact which is evident in every frame.

And don't even get me started on X-Men: First Class!

If you've seen that movie, I have a simple question for you: How the fuck did they get off the island? Seriously. At the end of the movie it's Professor X, his human girlfriend, the guy who shoots energy, the guy who can ... uh, scream really loud, Beast and that's it. They're trapped on a small island. They're surrounded by Russian and American ships full of humans who want them dead. HOW THE FUCK DID THEY ESCAPE? None of them have powers that could have enabled all of them to escape. And the humans are hostile, so they weren't rescued. What the fuck happened?

Perhaps I'm nit-picking, but that's a pretty big plot hole to forgive when nothing else in the movie works.

Charles (Professor X) and Erick (Magneto) are somewhat developed as characters, but the other characters are flat as pancakes. And this might be acceptable if they were at least superficially cool—but their mutant powers suck dead dog dick. A girl with dragonfly wings who spits molten cum? A guy who can yell ... really loud? A guy who can fire a laser . . . out of his chest? Meanwhile, the black guy who actually has the cool power of rapid evolutionary adaptations is killed unceremoniously in about two minutes.

The philosophical difference between Charles and Erick is supposedly the focal point of the film—but Charles makes no good case for his point of view. Erick's point of view is continuously vindicated by circumstance, whereas nothing in the film's dialogue, events or subtext gives any support to Charles' view whatsoever. So, remind me again why we're rooting for this guy? Why is he the protagonist?

And while I'm on the subject of things in movies that piss me off, I'd like to devote at least one paragraph to a disgusting phenomenon I've noticed cropping up all over the place in recent movies. I call it the "APPROVE OF ME, DADDY!" phenomenon. You know that scene in movies (and books) where the father/father-figure says, "I'm proud of you" for the first time and it's supposed to be this big emotionally powerful moment of release, where the protagonist has finally pleased his stodgy old father/father-figure? Am I the only one who finds such scenes pathetic? I understand why it appeals to people—but instead of fulfilling people's desires to please paternal authority figures, why don't we instead teach them to be satisfied with their own accomplishments, even if they don't ultimately get that validation?

Not all complaints against modern movies are valid, however. For instance, on the blogging site Tumblr, a faction of politically correct (and in no other way correct) people began to light their virtual torches and brand their virtual pitchforks because the Pixar film, 'Brave,' set in 10th century Scotland, didn't feature any African American characters. I wrote this refutation at the time:

So, apparently, there are some black people complaining about the lack of black people in Pixar's new movie Brave. So, here is what I'd like those black people to do. I'd like them to go to Google Image Search and type in Pixar Meeting or Pixar Team. Look at all the pictures. Who do you see? White people. Sure, there's the occasional Asian or Hispanic. But, mostly, it's white people.

Do you know why white people make movies about white people? Probably for the same reason black people make movies about black people. Black Directors like Spike Lee and Tyler Perry make movies about black people, not out of racism, but because that's who they are and that reflects their experience. But somehow when white filmmakers load their movies up with white characters, we're assholes? Racists? This is a double standard.

Here's my suggestion: if you're a black person who is furiously angry that black people aren't included in Brave, then you go get to college for years to study animation, get good enough to get hired by Pixar, work with them and their team, earn the respect of those around you, then say, "Hey. I think this character should be black." And *lay out a compelling case for why.*

Is that too hard? Well, it wasn't too hard for all those white people who work at Pixar now. They did the work. They control the art.

If you don't like it, then don't go see it. You want to change it? Then change it by creating something of your own or working to change the current system from within.

But, If all you're willing to do about your convictions is moan like babies, then fuck you. I don't care and I don't see any compelling reason why anyone else should care either.

Does racism still exist in America? Sure. Do white people like me have advantages? Yes. And you know what? We're not gonna give them up. We're NEVER going to give you a fair deal. And it's not out of malice. It's not out of racism. It's simply because we'll never see the problems in the system the way you do. There's no urgency to us, because we're inherently selfish. If the problem doesn't effect us, then we don't even see a problem.

So, If you want to fix the problems in this country that affect you, looking to us to fix them is a waste of time. You've got to fix them yourselves. And the way you do that is not by whining on

Tumblr. It's by dedicating yourself to your dreams and following them relentlessly until you've made the world a better place.

That's actually the only thing that anyone—regardless of race, gender, sexual orientation, whatever—can do. And if you think you can subvert that, you're delusional. I know the path is harder for you than it is for me, but the path doesn't get any easier. I'm sorry that being black is often like living life in Hard Mode. I'll never understand your struggles or what you go through, and I'm not even going to bullshit you about it.

But I know one thing: no amount of you complaining about how unfair things are is ever going to balance the equation. If that strategy really worked, wouldn't it have worked by now?

Addendum: A lot of commenters are asking "Well, why would there be black people in 10th century Scotland anyway?" There is a small percentage (0.16%) of black Scots in present times, and they have apparently been there for quite a few generations. Whether they stretch back to the 10th century is not something I know, nor is it something I care enough about to research.

But historical accuracy aside, plausibility is

not really an issue here. 'Mulan' was set entirely in China, and yet they still managed to shoehorn Eddie Murphy in there. It can be done. Though, in fairness, he was a dragon in that movie, not a black man.

The other comment I've seen arising is that black people have gotten certain rights and privileges by complaining in the past. No. They got them by demonstrating, conducting campaigns of civil disobedience, participating in highly organized boycotts, etc. It's not the same thing.

Of course, there are times when I find myself siding with the PC pussies, such as in the case of Orson Scott Card.

When I was young, I read a book called 'Ender's Game' by Orson Scott Card and so, I'm sure, have many of you. It's a very popular book among young adults (and adult-adults as well, I'm sure). It is, in my opinion, a very good book. I'm not alone in believing this. It has 2,400 five star reviews on Amazon. It won both the Nebula Award and the Hugo Award (prestigious in sci-fi circles). And next year, 'Ender's Game' the movie is set to come out, featuring Harrison Ford.

This is a book that meant something to me as a kid. It was empowering in a lot of ways, with its themes of unashamed intelligence, looking outside of the box, persevering against adversity and finding your own power through thought and calculated action.

The problem: the aforementioned author, Orson Scott Card, is a completely homophobic asshole. This is not the case of the guy making an off-color joke and the LGBT crowd taking it too seriously. This is not a case of him being misconstrued or misinterpreted in any way. He is proudly homophobic.

He called gay marriage, "The end of democracy."

He is on the board of NOM (An activist group dedicated to fighting gay marriage).

He actually said this: "Laws against homosexual behavior should remain on the books, not to be indiscriminately enforced against anyone who happens to be caught violating them, but to be used when necessary to send a clear message that those who flagrantly violate society's regulation of sexual behavior cannot be permitted to remain as acceptable, equal citizens within that society."

He is a man who is, at best, confused. At worst, evil. And I've bought at least three of his books. Can I, in good conscience, ever buy another one? Can anyone, in good conscience, see the movie based on his work? Do we judge the art by the sins of the artist, especially when said artist is still alive and profiting directly from our purchases? Or does art stand alone, separate from the flaws of the artist?

My conclusion is this: FUCK ORSON SCOTT CARD. I hope he dies soon so that I can buy his books without imagining some of my money going to him.

I'd like to shift our focus back to music, if I may. I have a controversial opinion on modern music and that opinion is this: contemporary music should be judged more by the quality of its lyrics than by the music itself.

This is not to say that I discard purely instrumental pieces. I have enjoyed many electronic pieces that incorporate little or no lyrical content whatsoever. Further, I acknowledge that a lot of music genres—metal, bluegrass, folk, alternative country, etc—do incorporate musical complexity that bears being judged on its own merits, regardless of lyrical quality. The level of artistry, precision and sheer emotional force renders certain musical pieces exceptional in and of themselves. But no one would listen to the music of Lady Gaga or even my hero Marilyn Manson by itself with no vocal/lyrical accompaniment. It would be incredibly monotonous and repetitive.

Most of the music that is popular is written to only be interesting with vocal accompaniment. So why should the vocal accompaniment be so banal? Why should people sing about such boring and bland topics? Why not infuse your lyrics with depth and meaning? Why not convey something important? How did we get from The Beatles, The Doors and The Rolling Stones to Justin Bieber, Nikki Minaj and Nickelback?

It is true that The Beatles started off as a boy band. But then they started experimenting with powerful psychoactive drugs and the music improved incredibly. The Beatles, The Doors and The Rolling Stones were all mainstream acts in their time. They were not under ground. You didn't have to dig around to find them. They were the mainstream. Now the mainstream is conspicuously devoid of anything as intelligent. We went from this:

> *The time to hesitate is through*
> *No time to wallow in the mire*
> *Try now we can only lose*
> *And our love become a funeral pyre*
> *Come on, baby, light my fire.*
> **The Doors, Light My Fire**

To this:

> *If I was your boyfriend, never let you go*
> *Keep you on my arm girl, you'd never be alone*
> *I can be a gentleman, anything you want*
> *If I was your boyfriend, I'd never let you go, I'd never let you go*
> **Justin Bieber, Boyfriend**

Am I the only one aware of this precipitous decline or am I just the only one who cares or sees it as culturally significant. Even beyond the mainstream, I have found very little worth justifying the existence of the generation's music. Perhaps you have some suggestions that could change my mind, but I doubt it. I've looked pretty extensively for new music that's worth a shit and come up empty-handed thus far.

To think, I used to feel like Limp Bizkit was the worst band ever. Fred Durst seems like a genius by modern standards. Everything is shit. Shallow, uninteresting, boring shit. I thought that the older generation was supposed to look at what the kids were listening to and think it too crazy and extreme. I look at what kids are listening to and think, "What a bunch of unimaginative little pussies."

Perhaps I'm just spoiled, however, since I grew up listening to the great, under appreciated lyrical master of our times: Marilyn Manson. A good understanding of lyrical content is far more vital for a Manson fan than it is for most fan bases (unless you're just some fan girl who wants to fuck him because he wears make-up—not that there's anything wrong with that). For instance, let's look at the lyrics to GodEatGod, the first track from the album Holy Wood (In the Shadow Of The Valley Of Death):

Dear god do you want to tear your knuckles down
And hold yourself
Dear god can you climb off that tree

Meat in the shape of a 'T'
Dear god the paper says you were the King
In the black limousine
Dear John and all the King's men
Can't put your head together again
Before the bullets
Before the flies
Before authorities take out my eyes
The only smiling are you dolls that I made
But you are plastic and so are your brains
Dear god the sky is as blue
As a gunshot wound
Dear god if you were alive
You know we'd kill you
Before the bullets
Before the flies
Before authorities take out my eyes
The only smiling are you dolls that I made
But you are plastic and so are your brains

If you're not aware beforehand that Manson is juxtaposing Jesus Christ and John F. Kennedy, then the lyrics can be a bit impenetrable. To fully understand the song, you have to know going in that "Meat in the shape of a T" is Christ on the cross. You have to know that "Dear John and all the King's men / can't put your head together again" refers to the Kennedy Assassination.

Why is Manson juxtaposing these two men? Because they're both revered figures in America who were made all the more famous because of their grizzly deaths. They're both martyrs.

The album's title, Holy Wood, is not just a play on Hollywood—it also refers to the tree of knowledge in the Garden of Eden, to the cross upon which Christ was crucified and to the wooden barrel of Lee Harvey Oswalt's rifle.

In Manson's own words, "I make references to the Zapruder film (of the Kennedy assassination) being the most important movie ever made in modern times. And the irony that anyone could complain about violence in films and entertainment when that was shown on the news. Growing up, I saw it so many times—and I've never seen anything so violent in my life. And that's reality. To me, Kennedy was a second Christ because he died and enough people were watching, and so [he] became a martyr."

Further: "It's strange that we accept the crucifix as if it were an everyday part of our household or a necklace to be worn. It's a very violent symbol, and if you think about how many people died in the name of that symbol, it's strange to wonder why the hammer and sickle is taboo or a swastika is taboo and the crucifix isn't."

Here's a song that's not even three minutes long that touches upon subjects that one could literally write entire books about. No one else in the history of pop culture can boast such complexity. So, if you want to get into Manson, don't think that you're just attempting to get into a new band. You're getting into a new way or perceiving the world around you.

But Marilyn Manson is old and his hayday is gone. I love his new work, but its cultural significance is negligible. And we can't get a new Marilyn Manson until we get a new Kurt Cobain. Cobain revitalized rock music after years of corporate decadence. He gave birth to alternative rock, and the next decade was a whirlwind of some of the bleakest and smartest music to penetrate the mainstream since the 1960's. But just as rock in the 70's took a backseat to meaningless Disco, rock today has taken a backseat to the pablum of pop and pseudo-hip-hop. Only electronic music today shows any promise of being intriguing. Most of the rock music coming out now is lifeless crap; a rehash of things done better a decade ago.

We need a new Cobain to shake things up. To usher in a new era. To make all this bland pop shit seem as fake to everyone else as it already does to me. You may say I'm a dreamer, but I'm not the only one.

Someone once posed to me a question: "When you're dying, do you want to look back on your life and only remember what a bunch of people on TV did?"

My reply was: Well, sure. If what they did was interesting. You have to remember when you make statements like this that everyone only gets one life and everyone has their choice of a few different paths. TV, at its best, sates our curiosity about other paths or other talents. You might be living your life to the fullest, making it big as a painter. That doesn't mean you can't enjoy an episode of House. *What if I were a medical genius instead of an artistic one?* Maybe you don't get the world's most accurate answer, but you get an answer. And it's enjoyable to watch.

If you think about it, your statement is really a criticism of empathy. To ask, "Why care about the people on TV, when you can instead focus on yourself?" is basically an advocacy of selfishness and isolation. Further, it's predicated upon a false notion—that concern for TV people is detracting from your own life. This isn't true. Human beings are defined by their interactions and their ability to perceive and interpret information. TV can enrich lives. So can music, painting, film, literature, theater, etc. The human condition grasps itself through individuals defining themselves via other individuals. The collective informs the man and the man, in turn, informs the collective.

In short, yes, when I'm dying, I want to look back on my life and remember what a bunch of people on TV did. What they did told me something about who I am.

People seem to think that our stories don't reflect us. They think that what we are entertained by isn't revealing of our character, but it is. Our values, ideas, thoughts and feelings will live on more in what we create artistically than anything else. And we are producing garbage.

Our young children are raised on Dora The

Explorer, Barney and other shows that promote values that we as human beings don't even seem to adhere to. I think societies values ought to be consistent. If we teach our children to share, be polite and have empathy, then we as adults should exemplify those values. If we will not (or cannot), then we should stop teaching those values to our children and instead teach them our true values: greed, selfishness and cynical detachment. Our teenagers play video games where the objective is no more inspiring than "shoot the generic threat." Our adults—well, we don't really have adults anymore, do we?

There's something I always wondered about John Carpenter's movie, 'The Thing' (1982): when the thing eats you and replicates you, including your memories, does the copy of you consciously know that it's the thing? This was never clear.

The obvious answer would seem to be yes, since the creature would attack when its charade was threatened, but I'm not so certain. What if the attack is a wholly unconscious act? A bacterial creature doesn't need consciousness to attack, consume or replicate.

Imagine it: you're sitting there with your

friends, scared shitless that one or more of them is a monster. And you don't have any idea that the real you died 45 minutes ago and that you're now just a replica created by an alien organism as a clever disguise.

Do you know what I thought during the recent prequel/remake of 'The Thing?' I thought, "This is fucking terrible." And it's not the first time I've had that thought sitting through a bad rehash or remake of a good film. What is it about this time and place that turns everything I love into shit? When did jump scares replace suspense? When did by-the-book homogeneity of thought and execution replace innovation and story telling? I'm not saying that everything new is bad and everything old was great—what I'm saying is that so much now is bad in exactly the same way. Because artists don't matter any more. The creative process of individual creators has been replaced by test audiences, market studies, simplifying plots for foreign markets, etc.

It seems like actors are picked for leading roles based on little more than their ability to have well-defined physiques and actresses are picked for supporting roles (almost exclusively supporting roles) based on how many men around the world will want to fuck them. It seems like scripts are chosen based on the fact that they are adaptations of something already successful or are remakes, sequels or rip-offs. Nothing original gets a bankroll.

And the same industries that give us this brain-numbing shlock are also the ones most keen on depriving us of our freedoms. SOPA and PIPA were born in Hollywood. And they will be reborn in Hollywood. The entertainment industry is never going to relent on its quest to deprive us of internet freedom. The entertainment industry is one of the scummiest industries around and their role in the increasingly shitty modern world we live in is greatly underestimated.

FEMINISTS (AND OTHER BORING PEOPLE TRYING TO SUCK THE LIFE AND JOY OUT OF THE WORLD)

The Feminists like to act as though rape jokes permeate our culture. "Rape jokes marginalize victims!" we are told. "They normalize rape! They give solace to rapists!" With all the anger directed at rape jokes, I've had a lot of time to reflect on just how many rape jokes there *aren't*.

Seriously, aside from two George Carlin rape jokes, neither of which I find very funny (nothing to do with being offended, they're just not great jokes), I can only think of a single rape joke:

4 out of 5 people enjoy gang rape.

This joke incorporates rape as an element. But I'm honestly not truly sure that you could really even consider this one a "rape joke." It's not making a joke about rape. It's just using rape for shock value. The joke is actually being made about the deceptiveness of statistics. The implication is, of course, that the 4 people out of 5 who like the gang rape are the rapists and 1 person who doesn't like it is of course the person being raped.

"4 out of 5 people" sets up a certain expectation. We hear this all the time. *5 out of 6 dentists recommend Crest! 3 out of 4 vets agree that Science Diet's patented formula leads to a healthier life for your pet! Etc.*

"Enjoy gang rape" takes our expectations and twists them. We're not going to the safe place we expected. We find ourselves going somewhere dark. The shock alone might induce a bit of nervous laughter.

But what really makes the humor work is that we see how the statement has a horrible technical truth to it. If four men are raping a woman or another man, they probably are enjoying themselves. And their victim is almost certainly not enjoying him- or herself.

This technical truth draws our focus back to the original expectation. We think to ourselves, "Maybe the methods of arriving at the conclusion that 5 out of 6 dentists recommend Crest is equally a "technical" truth rather than a "true" truth.

So, the focus on the joke is really more on statistics, and the way people use them to mislead, than it is about rape. The gang rape component is only included because it's a dark and shocking example of how a statistic might be manipulated or how our perceptions of reality might be misled by the careful omission of certain data.

The most recent rape joke controversy that got the feminazi saber-rattlers in a tizzy was when comedian Daniel Tosh fired back at a heckler by saying that she should be raped or that someone in the audience should rape her. Predictably, the feminists were offended and called for Tosh's head on a platter.

First of all, don't heckle a comedian. It's extremely disrespectful to try to fuck with someone else when they're doing a job. Daniel Tosh doesn't come to burger king and knock the fries out of your hands when you try to hand them to customers—so why would you try to fuck up his set?

Second of all, do people even understand what humor is? Do you know why George Carlin joked about war and human stupidity and suicide? Do you know why Louis C.K. jokes about the subtle despairs of modern life? Do you know why everyone jokes about Michael Jackson molesting little boys?

It's because laughter is one of the only tools human beings have to turn life's tragedies into something positive. Laughter is a shield against the darkness. Laughter is human beings trudging up to their own misery and spitting in its eye.

Rape is horrific, traumatizing and tragic. That's why we joke about it (and as I said before, not even very much)! Of course watching a rape isn't funny. Nor is it funny that human beings are oafs and brutes who slaughter one another, but that topic has never been taboo for satirists, commentators and other humorists.

People who make rape jokes are not endorsing rape. Saying that a joke about rape can be funny or acceptable is not even in the same ballpark as saying that rape is funny or acceptable.

Some feminists even go so far to say that joking about rape is, in and of itself, an act of violence. This is preposterous! A rape joke in not a violent act. Violence is when someone affects another person by physically doing something to their body that they do not want done. Rape is an act of violence. Punching someone is an act of violence. Shooting someone's dick off is an act of violence. Telling a joke, even an off-color one, is not an act of violence.

It seems that many feminists are of the opinion that rape is far worse than any other form of violence. A girl getting raped is worse than murder. They believe that. And they are shocked—outraged!—that anyone would think differently. In their view of the world, talking about rape isn't just words and ideas, it's a violent act in and of itself.

It is impossible to discuss the subject of rape without addressing some controversial comments that I made on reddit some time ago (that nonetheless continue to haunt me).

COMMENT #1: "I will make you a rape victim if you don't fuck off."

Oh my god? Did The Amazing Atheist really threaten someone with rape? No. No, he didn't. The full context of the remark was nothing to do with rape and everything to do with this strange new internet phenomena of "triggers." Some people now ask for "trigger warnings" if you post something the least bit incendiary, because your dangerous words may be detrimental to those with debilitating mental issues or emotional trauma.

I'm as sympathetic towards those who've suffered trauma as anyone else, but if you have such issues, it's your responsibility to avoid triggers, not my responsibility to protect you from them.

My comment was meant to make a point about how silly the concept of triggers is, and I made that clear several times in the thread when I said: "That was a joke, by the way. Did it trigger you?"

Did the feminists ever provide that context? Of course not. I may be an insensitive asshole—but I didn't legitimately threaten to rape someone. That is just stupid.

I will admit to some wrong doing. The comment I made afterward was pretty ugly. At the time it just seemed edgy, but in the light of morning I can see that I did myself no favors by typing it.

COMMENT #2: "Yeah. Well, you deserved it. So, fuck you. I hope it happens again soon. I'm tired of being treated like shit by you mean little cunts and then you using your rape as an excuse. Fuck you. I think we should give the guy who raped you a medal. I hope you fucking drown in rape semen, you ugly, mean-spirited cow. Actually, I don't believe you were ever raped! What man would be tasteless enough to stick his dick into a human cesspool like you? Nice gif of a turd going into my mouth. Is that kind of like the way that rapists dick went in your pussy? Or did he use your asshole? Or was it both? Maybe you should think about it really hard for the next few hours. Relive it as much as possible. You know? Try to recall: was it my pussy or my ass?"

I deeply regret going in that direction. I was trying

to make my point about triggers by writing the most "triggering" paragraph I possibly could. I should have at least provided some context. It was poor wording on my part and I sincerely apologize to anyone hurt by it. Yet again, it was immediately followed up by another post explaining my intentions. Yet again, feminists ignore this in favor of their assertion that I am pro-rape and anti-female.

Some off-color remarks said in the midst of a heated internet flame war are not to be taken seriously. And certainly not to be used as a be-all-end-all refutation to anything I have to say on the subject of feminism.

PZ Myers, popular blogger and self-appointed king of reason, had this to say: "This guy jokes about rape, threatens rape, and doesn't seem to recognize the line between consensual sexual activities and the violent act of rape. He's amazingly self-centered; he complains bitterly about the limits on his desires to put his penis where ever he wants as an awful example of feminism controlling his sexuality, completely oblivious to the fact that what he ultimately wants to do is control other people's sexuality, putting it in service to his fantasies."

What PZ Myers obviously is unaware of is that

I am a submissive who places the pleasure of my wife/owner far above my own. Well, actually, it's more accurate to say that giving her pleasure is what gives me pleasure. But who I actually am is of no consequence—feminists like PZ Myers would rather debate a straw man than address my actual arguments. Is this because they're stupid cowards? Yes. Yes, it is.

Am I biased here? Perhaps I am. But my experience has been that every feminist I've ever spoken to has wanted me to make concessions that I'm uncomfortable with—not because I don't like their implications, but because the foundation of the arguments that they are predicated upon seem weak to me.

For instance, have you ever noticed that rape is one of those issues where we're discouraged from looking at multi-faceted answers?

Don't get me wrong, blaming a girl's flirtatious nature or revealing outfit for her rape is repugnant and, worse, inaccurate. However, just declaring, "rapists are evil," and never examining anything beyond that assumption seems equally ignorant.

We know that rates of rape are different from society to society. We know that what constitutes rape is different from society to society. We know that attitudes towards victims of rape are different from society to society. So why can't we have a frank discussion concerning the anthropology of rape, the sociology of rape, the sociobiology of rape, the psychology of rape, etc.?

Why do we have to settle for easy answers and applaud the safe, morally-delineated-to-the-maximum-degree pablum of the feminists?

To be fair to the feminist point of view, accountability does, at the end of the day, rest on the shoulders of the rapist. But we're in denial if we think that environmental factors, genetic abnormalities, mental illnesses, societal attitudes, belief systems, legal systems, particular subcultures, etc., don't have an impact. If they didn't, you'd see far greater parity in the rates of rape from one place to another.

There's no way to stop rape effectively and permanently if we refuse to take a sober look at the phenomena and what actually causes it. And the first step is to demythologize the rapist; to look at rapists as human beings being driven by impulses rather than monsters powered by evil.

A rational society would give those with these

urges a place to go to talk address their feelings with professional help—instead the very feelings that cause rape are taboo. Those who experience said feelings are treated as pariahs if they give voice to their feelings. Doesn't this only put them at risk of offending? Doesn't this current attitude remove the very societal constraints that might have stopped our hypothetical rapist from raping? If you are a monster just for wanting to do it—then why not go ahead and do it?

We can't continue treating people like monsters and then wondering why they have so few reservations about doing monstrous things.

One of the frequently brought up feminists arguments when this topic is broached pertains to childhood victims of rape and sexual abuse. Surely I don't blame children for getting raped? No. Nor do I blame adult victims of rape for being raped. The entire notion that I, or any reasonable person, blames rape victims for their rapes is a giant straw man that emerges solely from the inability of certain people to allow any nuance into this issue whatsoever.

The feminist have created a dogma—and part of that dogma is the following absolute: the victim is totally blameless in all ways, at all times and under all circumstances. Failure to accept this premise unquestioningly and without reservation or exception makes you a "victim-blamer" in the eyes of certain segments of the feminist community.

Children are, of course, entirely blameless in their victimization because they lack power, experience and autonomy. If mommy or daddy decides to sneak into his or her child's bedroom, what recourse does said child have at its disposal to prevent the rape they are about to endure? What preventative measures could the child have taken? What ability did the child have to even recognize or understand the threat? No one could conceivably pin any responsibility for a sexual assault on a child victim. That would be absurd.

Adults are not similarly powerless, however. There are preventative measures that they can take.
- Take classes in basic defensive techniques
- Carry a weapon
- Avoid walking home alone, especially in certain areas.
- Make sure someone always knows where you are

I've heard women (and men, to a lesser degree)

say to me, "I shouldn't have to do those things! They impinge on my freedom!" My response to that is that I fully agree that women should not have to do these things. They should be able to walk the streets alone without the slightest fear that a rapist is stalking them. They should be able to walk about unarmed without concern. They should be able to conduct themselves as they see fit without having to consider who might be plotting to rape them.

The world, however, does not give a fuck about how you or I think it should be. I don't think I should have to buy an alarm for my home—people should just respect my personal property and not attempt to steal from me! However, that's not how the world works. I have to take scumbags, liars and thieves into account everyday and adjust my conduct accordingly. Why should rape be exempt from taking precautions against?

Now, if I get robbed, beaten or swindled, is it my fault if I didn't take the proper precautions? No. However, if you let me off the hook completely, where is the lesson? Am I to be excused entirely for my lack of preparedness simply because it was ultimately up to the burglar or attacker to act against me? Is it really so wrong to simply make note of what a victim could have done better? Is it really so heinous to simply suggest that victims should be aware of risks and take reasonable precautions?

A rape victim, of course, suffers more trauma than a victim of robbery. Having your house violated can be chilling, but having your body violated is several orders of magnitude beyond that. However, the emotional pain caused by rape is immaterial when it comes to assessing the responsibilities of potential victims to safeguard themselves. If anything, the severity of the trauma involved is all the more reason why stressing the importance of rape prevention is paramount.

Of course, personal preventative measures are a small part of rape prevention. Far more important is changing societies attitude towards rapists from evil to impaired and setting up a net to identify the character traits of rapists before they rape and urging them into treatment.

No one on this planet should have to suffer rape. And I believe that rape can largely be stopped, but only if we accept it for what it is and work from there, rather than basing policies on moral outrage and politically correct indignation.

Many feminists say that our society shouldn't

teach women not to get raped, but should teach men not to rape. I don't think that we should teach either sex anything like that.

We won't eliminate rape by making girls and women so afraid that they're going to get raped that they become neurotic worrywarts who can barely function because they're so frightened that men are nothing but a gaggle of rape-hungry fiends.

Nor will we eliminate rape by merely proscribing it and admonishing those who commit it. Rapists are already hated, shunned, castigated, imprisoned and looked down upon by the whole of society. There are movies out there where the protagonists are hitmen, mafiosos and even serial killers—but when is the last time you saw a movie or TV show where a rapist was the hero? When is the last time you read a flattering news article about a rapist? When is the last time you heard a friend say, "Yeah. That's my buddy, Charles. He's a rapist, but he's still pretty cool." Despite feminist cries about how we live in a "rape culture" there is actually nothing about our culture that sends the message to anyone that it's okay to be a rapist.

The way that we can eliminate rape is by treating the underlying causes of rape. We need to fund a lot of research into understanding the mentality of rapists and what causes them to act out so that we can identify at risk behaviors and attitudes before they offend. We can prevent victims with higher awareness and rational compassion.

A popular feminist argument is to say that the opinions of people like me need not be taken seriously or addressed because I have a number of "privileges". I have what they would label "male privilege" and "white privilege."

Privilege, as it is used by feminists, is an entirely meaningless term. It's a mantra that they spout like dolls with broken draw strings: MALE PRIVILEGE! MALE PRIVILEGE! MALE PRIVILEGE! YOUR OPINION IS INVALID BECAUSE YOU HAVE MALE PRIVILEGE!

I think the reason that they're so fond of citing male privilege is because they have no argument beyond acting persecuted.

The term doesn't even make sense. What does it mean to have male privilege? What exactly is my privilege? Peeing standing up?

And what of female privilege? What of the fact that men disproportionately lose custody battles for children? What of the fact that male victims of domestic or sexual abuse are not taken seriously by society as a whole? Feminists actually do admit that examples like this are sexism—sexism against women.

They argue that male victims of domestic abuse are only not taken seriously because women are considered weak. They argue that women only win more custody battles because women are viewed as natural caregivers.

When a stereotype favors men over women, it's sexism against women. When a stereotype favors women against men . . . it's still sexism against women? If you're confused, you obviously don't know how feminism works. Allow me to explain: if there is an issue where men have it better than women, such as the fact that male athletes are paid better and watched more, then that's because males run the world and we're maliciously working to suppress women at all times.

If there is an issue where women have it better than men, such as the fact that we're far more likely to be ruled against in child custody suits, then that's because males run the world and we're maliciously working to suppress women at all times.

It makes a lot of sense if you don't think about it.

I want to make something clear. I love women. I am not threatened by femininity. I am not frightened of female expression or female sexuality. I am not trying to get women into the kitchen to be barefoot and pregnant while making me a sandwich. I want women to be every bit as free to explore their lives and desires as men are. Which is why I am opposed to feminism.

One of the worst things about feminism is that a lot of it—not all—while claiming to empower women, is really far more concerned with selling women on the idea that they are powerless and oppressed. For instance, feminism is eager to constantly bemoan the lack of female engineers. "Engineering is a male dominated field!" they shout.

But when you inquire with them further, their line of reasoning is shaky. They think engineering is male-dominated because there aren't many female engineers and they think there aren't many female engineers because engineering is male-dominated.

FEMINIST: Did you know that only 11% of

engineers are women!

ME: Oh? That sucks. Why don't more women become engineers?

FEMINIST: Because it's a male-dominated industry.

ME: Well, the more women become engineers, the less male-dominated it will be.

FEMINIST: They can't become engineers until the engineering field is less male-dominated!

ME: So . . . more women can't become engineers until the engineering field is less male-dominated?

FEMINIST: Right.

ME: And the engineering field can't become less male-dominated until more women become engineers?

FEMINIST: Right.

ME: Well, good luck with that.

If, instead of whining about a lack of female engineers, feminists merely empowered women by letting them know, "YOU CAN BE AN ENGINEER (or whatever else you want to be)" then these fields would no longer be male-dominated. You can't say, "It's male-dominated because there are no women and there are no women because it's male-dominated." You've stalemated yourself.

Feminism too often teach women to be content with complaining about problems instead of working to solve them. My message, by contrast, is that you solve problems by solving problems, not by endlessly pointing out that the problems exist and expecting others to address them for you.

The only time when that is justified is when there are concrete legal barriers that need surmounting. But as far as I know, there isn't a law stating that females can't be engineers. So, feminists who are bitching about the lack of female engineers should get engineering degrees instead of degrees in Women's Studies.

I'd like to share with you a true story of male privilege that I wrote a while back:

I was walking down the street when I saw this girl with gigantic tits walking the other way. I began to drool. I began to fondle imaginary breasts in the air. I began to hump the air in front of me.

The girl, disgusted, accosted me: "Hey! Disgusting male pig! I grow sick of your male privilege! I am not a sex object!"

"Oh?" I said. "I disagree. An object is defined as 'anything that is visible or tangible and is relatively stable in form.' You clearly meet the definition of an object. And since, from a biological standpoint, all human beings exist to propagate their genetic code via sexual reproduction, you are, in fact, a sex object."

Stunned by the power of my logic, she got to her knees and blew me.

True story.

One of my biggest problems with the privilege line of rhetoric is that privilege is so completely relative. When you say "white privilege," for example, it makes an assumption that whites have more privileges than blacks (or other racial groups). But, obviously, a white person living in rural

Arkansas probably doesn't have more privilege than a black banker in New York City—privilege isn't a big tent that all of the subsets of a set stand under.

There's also a question of cause and effect at play: do white people have more privilege because they have more wealth, or do they have more wealth because they have more privilege?

Then there's a question of how to quantify privileges: how does male privilege stack up to female privilege? Certainly, there are areas where women are advantaged over males, and vice versa. How do we measure different sets of privileges against one another?

It's not really as simple as some people wish it were. A lot of people who make the "privilege" argument want it to be "GROUP X HAS MORE PRIVILEGE THAN GROUP Y THEREFORE GROUP X IS EVIL."

We need to move away from that sort of argument, and start addressing the need for people to be treated as individuals, not merely as extensions of groups we perceive them as belonging to.

But such an approach would require modern feminism to make concessions, and that's something that they simply will not do. The way feminists look at things is that half the country is female, and males really don't have the power they once did, so women don't have to really care about extending the olive branch any more. Their attitude is pretty much, "We will only accept non-females into our fold if they prostrate themselves before us! KNEEL, MALE SCUM, AND KISS THE RING. I AM THE FEMINIST POPE AND I WILL PURGE THIS WORLD OF NONBELIEVERS!"

They know that we're not going to do anything about it. So what's to stop them? There are plenty of women who hate men, hate masculinity and hate masculine values. And they codify their bigotry as part of an ideology to make it acceptable.

They're a bunch of KU KLUX KUNTS.

Most human beings haven't really caught up to the fact that bigotry has evolved. Rednecks sitting on couches hating blacks and Mexicans is passe. They're still out there—but they're no longer empowered. They're a withered group of deflated, defeated, bitter men.

The feminazis, however, are empowered. And they're organized. And they have mainstream acceptability. They hide behind the guise of equality, but what they really stand for is the solidification of a new double standard that they promote, wherein female values reign supreme over male ones.

It's just another group of people looking for as much power as they can get—human nature as usual.

All groups strive for power. For some, power is desperately out of reach. For others, they're positioned just right. I think modern feminism is poised for big things. I think they're going to get a lot more control, especially in academic circles. We've already seen them hijack and conquer new atheism, implementing draconian, male-blaming rules for atheist conventions—led in their charge by the aforementioned PZ Myers and the in(s)ane bigot Rebecca Watson, more popularly known as The Skepchick (she hosts a relatively popular podcast and is a horrendous human being who's misandry is outweighed only by her ego).

And what of female privilege when it comes to reproductive rights? Think about this: Two people have unprotected sex. Oops! They *both* made the exact same mistake.

Here are choices a woman can make after that mistake to abdicate herself of responsibility:

- The girl can take the morning after pill.

- She can take the one week pill.
- If she gets pregnant, she can get an abortion.
- If she gives birth to an unwanted baby, she can legally abandon it at the hospital in most states. Or she can give it up for adoption.

Here are choices a man can make after that mistake to abdicate himself of responsibility:

-
-
-
-

That's why I think that a man should be able to say, "I forfeit all responsibility for this child, but also all rights to this child." Women have several outs. Men deserve at least one. The concept is called financial abortion, and I am a proponent.

We can't talk about feminism properly if we fail to delve into the feminist complaint that media is saturated with a particular body image and female aesthetic that girls and women are pressured to conform to.

I think the impact of such things has been exaggerated. We've always depicted beauty in art, and it makes sense that our affinity for the lovely would carry over into advertising. Why would you use an "ugly" person to sell something?

People say, "Oh! It gives girls an unrealistic body image!" So? That's what beauty is, right? When someone looks exceptionally aesthetically pleasing to many people. Girls who can't come to terms with not being beautiful are shallow. And their attempts to control the media to stop the tyranny of beauty are even more shallow.

I am an ugly fuck. I don't sit around whining about Brad Pitt giving me an inferiority complex with his alluring smile and excellent physique. Or crying that porn stars should have smaller dicks because I feel inadequate when I see well hung guys.

But you can't win an argument with feminists. No matter what you say to them you are just a "dudebro" or a "neckbeard" with "male privilege" and you're part of "the patriarchy."

The patriarchy is the secret cabal of males who make sure women stay good and oppressed. Fit fathers who lose custody of their children to unfit mothers—it's your own fault for supporting the patriarchy! If only you'd have realized that you're a piece of male scum unworthy of being spit on, then you'd be able to raise your son.

It doesn't have to make sense. It's feminism.

THE STINKING GODDAMN HUMAN CONDITION AND OTHER MEANINGLESS CONCERNS

Let's talk about humanity. But first, let's talk about my perspective on humanity so that you know where I'm coming from.

The more I assess the world lately, the more I feel like a Martian sent by my home planet to survey a dying culture and take notes. The problem is that I know I'm not a Martian. I am witnessing the slow collapse of my own culture, and I'm unsure of what actions I should take to contravene this outcome. The realization—the understanding—is that I am powerless to affect the outcome of the human experiment.

Carl Sagan postulated that if the Drake Equation was correct, the most likely reason why we'd never encountered or been contacted by an advanced alien race is because all societies that reach our level of technological advancement end up destroying themselves. Nothing going on in the world right now is very reassuring against Sagan's hypothesis.

How can I continue to make videos about a world whose prospects seem as dim as a burnt out light bulb? How can I put passion into my words, when all I feel in my heart is a deep malaise that resembles surrender? I feel like a louse in the hair of a dying hobo, screaming to the other lice that the hobo is dying. What a useless waste of effort.

Yet, YouTube butters my bread. And I've got a new project—Not Productive—that will require much of my formerly free time. I am attempting to build a future for myself—in a world that I think has no future. It's hard to see the point, some days. I feel like Steve Buscemi's character, Garland Green. in the stupid but enjoyable action flick *'Con-Air'*: ironically singing a children's song while aboard a crashing plane, certain of the impending disaster and yet unmoved by its supposed importance.

So you have to remember that when I look at humanity, my natural tendency is to look at it as though I were an alien being who has no stake in it. I think we are the most interesting species on this planet by a huge margin. We have the widest variety of the most interesting behaviors.

When I watch a nature documentary, I don't judge the Lion for eating cute little Cheetah cubs. I don't judge the female spider for eating the male after mating. I don't judge ants for waging plunder campaigns against termites. I don't judge female gorillas for eating the offspring of competitor females. This is just nature. Nature is full of very naughty and cruel behavior.

Human beings have no magical exemption from this. If anything, due to our complexity, we are more prone to odder and deeper cruelty and viciousness. We are also more prone to very bizarre sexual behaviors that run the gamut from silly to sadistic.

Just as I don't judge animal behaviors, I don't judge human ones either. There is no action that a person can take, other than one directly effecting myself or my sphere of friends, that will cause me to judge them harshly. However, while I don't judge individual humans for their odd transgressions, I do have some judgments to dole out to the species as a whole.

There's a popular quotation by Edmund Burke that, "All that is necessary for evil to triumph is for good men to do nothing."

I think it's the other way around. I think that for good to be triumphant, evil men would have to do nothing. Think about it: if you've got a group of people, and they're all evil but one, the one can't stop the rest from being evil. He can try, but they'll just kill him. Or torture him. Or rape him in the ass and feed his spleen to gophers. The good man did something. He failed. Evil triumphed.

Now let's say the reverse is true. Everyone is good, but one man is evil. All the evil person has to do is distort the truth to make his evil seem like good. Human history is full of this type of person—Hitler, Mao, Stalin, Amin, etc. Good men rose up against

Hitler, but he still managed his genocide. In fact, he tricked a lot of good men into carrying his evil out. Because he was deceitful and manipulative—which are hallmarks of evil. They're part of the nature of evil.

Evil is simply better equipped to win, regardless of the numbers game. Even a simplistic form of evil like the Columbine shooters, Eric Harris and Dylan Klebold, have an advantage over good. They walked into their school and killed their classmates. No one could stop them. They killed lots of people who were, presumably, good. No matter how you slice it, evil won that day. And evil won again when more complex villains with media and political power turned kids like me (I was about 14 when Columbine went down) into a scapegoat for America's problems. People remember that the media blamed Marilyn Manson. But everyone forgets that the media and the politicians also put a target on the back of every kid that dressed or acted differently from their peers.

All that is necessary for good to triumph is for evil men to do nothing.

Humanity is fucked. Our technology has outpaced our intellect. We still make decisions like cavemen, because the results of our decisions probably never used to have an impact beyond our own tribe. Now, we live in a world where knowledge is freely available to anyone with access to Google, and instead of using that, we seek out trivial distractions.

We live in a world where it would only take one unstable psychopath with high-level access in the world government or corporation to unleash a mega-virus or detonate a dirty bomb in Times Square.

Our situation is unstable, and it's something of a miracle that we haven't destroyed ourselves already.

For instance, did you know that the Soviet Union created, and the current Russian government CONTINUES TO MAINTAIN, a weapon that will send hundreds of nuclear missiles our way if there is a nuclear attack on Russia? What if it's accidentally set off by an earthquake? What if Iran bombs Russia, knowing that in doing so they will assure the total annihilation of America? This is a huge problem that our leaders know about . . . and yet don't even address!

Sometimes people get on my case about this

sort of thinking. They say, "Why don't you care about the fate of humanity?" My reaction is that humanity is a piece of shit. What's to care about? There's plenty to fascinate me about my species, but very little to endear me to it.

Humanity at its worst is a bunch of murderous war-mongering jackals and rapists. Crack open a history book or turn on CNN. You might have to wait a while on CNN. They'll probably tell you about some bimbo actress' latest dress long before they tell you the latest death toll in Syria.

Humanity at its best is a bunch of simple-minded assholes who are so misinformed that they think that voting means something. Obama or Romney? That's not a drastic policy choice. That's a superficial choice, and any intellectually honest person knows it. This is yet another American election where you have to choose between the authoritarian right and the slightly less authoritarian right.

The majority of Americans accept this blatantly false dichotomy as an exercise in freedom. And it's no different in most other countries. The UK still has monarchs rattling around, for fuck's sake.

"But, TJ, the monarchy doesn't have any real

power." Well, congratulations on that. You've managed to pay for, with your tax dollars, people who do nothing except attend ceremonies and live in the lap of luxury. Why? Because they came out of a royal pussy instead of a peasant pussy. Yeah. You're so fucking enlightened.

"But, TJ, we make a lot in tourist money from people coming to see the royal family." Yes. You've turned your antiquated system into a tourist trap. You must be so proud.

Fuck humanity. If you want my concern so much, then explain to me how you're worth it. And don't throw Beethoven or Einstein at me. Those people are ridiculously exceptional. They are not an accurate representation of humankind as a whole.

Part of the problem is that our evolution never really prepared us to handle modern living—we didn't develop to interact with faceless masses, but with the familiar faces of our tribe! And people still seek out tribes, because they don't want to feel isolated in the sea of the unfamiliar.

But part of the strength of a true tribe is that it's a group of people working together despite a variety of opinions. Different perspectives within the same group leads to a system where everything is considered from many different angles.

But that doesn't work when everyone picks their own tribe. People tend to surround themselves exclusively with other people who agree with them.

So our modern tribes—from the religious right to the PC left—have no ideological diversity. They purposely screen *against* ideological diversity. So, we've really all become ideological cheerleaders in a never ending war for purity and supremacy. Cooperation? Overcoming differences? Ha! That's so yesterday!

People need to grow up. There are 7 billion of us. We're not all going to have good lives. We're not all going to get what we want. We're not all going to be treated fairly. I think the first step towards the best possible society is admitting that no society is going to be anywhere vaguely near perfect. We can't write bullies, bigots and bad people out of the script. And we certainly can't get anywhere worth going if we only associate with our own ideological clones.

We are just a tragic species! People build empires because their fathers didn't love them enough. People kill prostitutes because they were too scared to ask girls out in high school. People shoot themselves in the head because no one understands them.

Human deeds can, no doubt, be monumental, encompassing the most vile of malicious deeds as well as the most selfless acts of charity.

But at the core of almost all human actions, there is a pathetic motive—usually something to do with a traumatic failure to connect with another person at some vital moment of raw need. We are always avenging our own loneliness. Even with 7 billion companions, we are lonely. Even with ideologically delineated groups, we feel as thought no one hears us.

Some ask why I am not an advocate of suicide if my view of humanity is so bleak. "What reason do we have not to kill ourselves immediately after we become aware of life's futility?" I am asked.

Because if there's anything more futile than life—it's death. In life, there is happiness, love, pleasure, conflict, excitement, terror—does it all boil down to essentially nothing? Pretty much.

But death *is* nothing. No happiness, love, pleasure, conflict, excitement, terror—nothing at all. You can't even be bored by it, because you will not exist and will therefore have no perspective or judgment. You won't even have a you.

Also, why rush to eternal nothingness? Why not enjoy the minuscule blink of life you've got? Why not fill it with something meaningful to you? If you want to get married and have kids, do that. If you want to stick bananas in your butt, do that too.

Personally, I have a woman I love, friends worth conversing with, sexual realms to explore, creative endeavors I can't wait to embark on and self-changes to enact.

I have things to live for.

Humanity cannibalizes it's own soul by working to abuse, oppress and subjugate those who stand out from the herd. If my happiness was tied to the human condition, I'd be miserable. But it's not! I don't play that game. I focus on myself and my passions, because that's the only way to stay sane in a world full of drones.

In other words, I try to remain detached from the spectacle of human failure. I don't always achieve this detachment, but usually I do. And it's how I attain personal happiness despite having an unflattering view of my species. It is my self-determination that makes me a content person.

Self-determination is the core human right. Without that, any other rights are essentially just nifty little fringe benefits of no substance. The concept of self-ownership means that you can conduct yourself as you see fit without the interference of conformity-enforcers who seek to legislate against your ability to choose for yourself. To say I own myself is to say that I am a piece of my own property and that my value is incalculable. To say that you own yourself is to say the same. If anyone else tries to steal your ability to self-determine, whether they are the government or a private citizen or a company—they are stealing from you. They are stealing ownership of your self from yourself. This is the most grievous possible outrage. The protection of self-ownership is the basis for my moral code.

For too long, we have allowed our government jurisdiction over our bodies. This is not, to me, a women's issue or a men's issue—this is an issue of all human beings. Your government has told you:

- When you're allowed to have sex.
- What kind of sex you're allowed to have.
- What drugs you can take and what drugs you can't.
- That you can't kill yourself, even if you're sick

and in horrible pain.
- That it's up to them whether or not you can have an abortion.

These are just a few obvious examples of the ways in which the government has declared that you are their property, not the property of yourself.

I believe that we are the owners of ourselves. We have inherent domain over our own bodies, and can therefore utilize our bodies in any manner we see fit, so long as we don't bodily harm another human being against their wishes. Therefore, I think that we should be completely allowed to amuse ourselves with whatever drugs we wish. Drugs affect the mind. They affect perception. To ban drugs is to ban certain ways of thinking and perceiving, which is quite Orwellian. I think that we should have sex when we want to, wear what we please, do as we see fit. It's as Aleister Crowley wrote, "Do what thou wilt shall be the whole of the law."

That's my moral code.

Actually, I dislike the concept of "moral." I prefer to think in terms of ethics. The difference (to me—and these are my personal definitions) is that a moral means a unit of behavioral control and ethic is an emotional or intellectual guideline to interpreting the values of different actions with a given situation.

Many people fear this way of thinking, seeing it as a slippery slope to wickedness. And it's true that If my sole ethical precept were, "My pleasure, above all else!" then they would have a point.

But I recognize that "the right to swing my fist ends where the other man's nose begins." In other words, I don't think it can be my right to infringe upon the rights of another person. If I had the right to infringe upon them, then they would have the right to infringe upon me—and the whole concept of rights would break down.

I believe that human beings should seek out happiness, as long as their happiness doesn't directly harm others who do not wish to be harmed.

This is actually the philosophy of many people, I think. It's hardly unique to me. Nor is it difficult to understand. Yet, it seems prone to encouraging intentional misinterpretation on the part of it's detractors—those who favor more rigid moral codes.

That said, I think human beings need order to thrive and that some people have difficulty coming to grips with that aspect of humanity. Anarchists of all stripes tote that, without central control, human beings would be saintly angels who would hold hands in brotherhood in a government-free utopia.

If anarchy is the best form of (the lack of) governance than is the best form of parenting to simply abandon your children in a dumpster so that they may fend for themselves? Is the best form of coaching a football team to allow the players to do whatever they wish with no overarching strategy to guide their actions?

No one truly believes that anarchy is a good idea. Anarchy is an emotionally satisfying solution to the problems inherent with authority. Their are more intellectual solutions that are both more effectual and more elegant—though less appealing!

I wasn't always content to separate myself from my species. There was a time, not long ago, when I felt more apprehensive about life in general, as the following blog post from a few years ago bears out:

Most people have some sense of confidence when it comes to their day to day lives. Don't get me wrong: they've got insecurities and all that, but when it comes to the daily grind they have some sense of purpose, some sense of direction. I lack that entirely. I can't deal with people. I can't handle social situations any more complicated than ordering food at a restaurant.

On the other hand, most people, when faced with a flight or fight situation, will run. People are cowards. I am not a coward. I will fight. Even if I know I will lose, I want to fight. I want to see if I can cheat defeat; defy odds, that jazz.

I know the reality is that I'm not strong for fighting. A strong man would know when to run. A strong man would also know when to stop fighting himself. But I am not strong. I feel at times like I am the epitome and apotheosis of all neurotic human weakness. And in my weakness, I am petty. And in my pettiness, I am a fighter. Not for a noble cause. Not even for self-preservation.

I fight because I have a narcissistic hatred of life and of myself. Every argument, large or small; every major criticism, every minor nitpick, every complaint, every grumpy frown or snide remark— it's all part of some mean-spirited vendetta I have against the world because I am personally unhappy and at odds with myself.

But I don't let myself feel that most days. Most

days, I focus on the hate. It's a lot better to hate than to despair. But then there are moments like these when they hate isn't large enough to drown out the truth: You are unhappy, TJ.

You always have been. You always will be. No matter what wealth or status you accrue, no matter how many people love and support you, no matter how many battles you win—you will always be unhappy. There's something wrong with your brain chemistry. You'll never stop tearing yourself apart. You'll never stop being your own worst critic.

I am so damn weary of it all. I'm so tired of living a life where I live in hatred and take long vacations in depression. I'm so tired of this mental dissonance that plagues me.

It's becoming unbearable.

The mistake I was making when I wrote that is that I was still judging myself on the basis of what society expected from me. I was still viewing the world as though I were owned by my culture, rather than being my own property. But I changed my perspective, as I am free to do.

The human experience is largely subjective, so rational thought still offers a wide variety of thought and opinion. It's not as if rational thought will cause us to coalesce into some beastly collective of twin-minded freaks who agree on everything.

The greatest gift we human beings have is our ability to choose to perceive the world differently than we've been instructed. We can even override our own predispositions with enough willpower! And as my friend, author Howard Bloom, often says, "new ways of seeing lead to new ways of being."

I have never aspired to change the world, simply because that task is beyond me. There are too many variables involved; too many disparate wills pushing and pulling the world in too many different directions. If I genuinely aspired to improve the world, I'd be crippled by depression, never able to shake from my head the inescapable conclusion that my efforts are exercised in futility. The world will not change because I tell it to, and even if it did change, I would have no control over the nature of that change.

Yet, if I realize that it's not my job to chance the world and that I'm only responsible for myself and my own actions, then I don't feel powerless any more. I don't feel like I'm a speck of dust, but the center of the universe. Because I am my own universe. And when I die, my mind is gone and my universe is gone with it. I know, objectively, that matter and energy will continue to exist long after my demise, but I don't need to concern myself with that too much. It's beyond my ability to affect or control and accepting that is far more sublime a feeling than wishing things were otherwise.

I've not, since adopting my new worldview, felt a tremendous need in myself for a deeper meaning. I'm a fairly worldly and hedonistic fellow who finds the pleasures of this plane of existence sufficient to sustain myself.

I think that many people like to wander through the desert of their own elaborate self-markers—grandiose little chunks of narrative that they plant into the ground to remind themselves of their perceived highs and lows. Plant a flag where I met my wife, plant a flag where my dog died, plant a flag where I started working an administrative job over a the offices of Penguin Publishing.

And they look back at the landscape, pocked with flags waving in the harsh dessert wind and they say to themselves, "I had a life. I had a self. These flags prove it."

But then the camera pans back and we discover

that the desert is vast beyond reckoning. And our protagonist, the flag-planting human being who affirms himself to the universe, has journeyed less than a millimeter across this barren wasteland's surface. The flags that he planted are microscopic.

Why then compare yourself to the desert? Why not compare yourself instead to the millimeter you have traveled and say, "Ah. It was a god millimeter. A good speck." Accepting insignificance and embracing limitation is so much more satisfying than aspiring to accomplish great things when you are too small and too temporary to truly do so.

Others find the value of their live in the concept of God. Religion. I don't address it too much in this book, but I will harken back to a series of questions I once asked about God.

What is God? Is it a what? Or is it a who? Is it an it? Is he a he? Is she a she?

Believers say that God is the entity that created creation. Everything you see is the work of God: trees, hills, bumble bees, pancakes, stars, chocolate pudding, lava, incandescent light bulbs. God made it all. He's a busy guy, if he is a guy, and if he exists, and if he is discernible to the human mind.

"God!" Is it just something to scream when we're mad or when we're cumming? Is he just someone to thank before every meal? Is she our mother earth, forests sewn into her skin like hairs and rivers covering her body like veins?

What is God? Maybe God is an if. If we don't know the answer, then the answer is God. If God makes us feel good, then God is real. If all my friends believe that there is a God, then there is a god.

Maybe God is a contingency plan; an ejector seat when reality becomes too difficult. Some say that God is manifest in the splendor of the universe. Why then is he not manifest in the squalor of the universe?

We say "God damn it!" when we stub our toe, as if God will hear us and smite the table that we stubbed it on. We say, "God willing," when we hope that God will intercede on the behalf of our cause. We say "God bless you," when someone sneezes, because apparently God cares a lot about the rapid expulsion of mucus from your nostrils. We say, "God help us," when doom approaches. We say, "Oh my God," when exasperation overtakes us. We say,

"Why, God?" when malady afflicts us. We say, "God works in mysterious ways" when what we really mean is that the universe acts in random and callous ways. We say, "God bless America," or "God save the Queen," or something similar to express our loyalty towards whatever government power lords over our lives. We say, "God is watching," to instill fear. We say, "God is good," as if to convince ourselves that this is true. We call the righteous men, "God-fearing."

Fearing God is righteous? "God-loving" is not a term that has yet entered the common vernacular, though God is sometimes referred to as a "Loving God."

We say, "In God we trust," but if that were true, then what use would we have for all these tanks and missiles. We say, "God helps those who help themselves." But those who help themselves don't need God's help.

What is God? Is God an X. A variable? A place marker?

God is that which we need God to be. A despot one moment, a redeemer the next. One who will love you, but send your enemies to roast in flames. One who is so great that he created the universe, yet so petty that he persecutes the homosexuals. One who explains everything that isn't explained, until someone else explains it.

Believers, I ask: is God you? Is God your biases? Is God your judgments? Is God your ego? Let's cut to the chase: Are you God?

When you say, "God damn this chair!" aren't you really the one damning the chair? When you say, "God Bless America!" aren't you really expressing your own love for America. When you say, "God doesn't approve of the sinners," aren't you really saying that you don't approve of someone, and so you've slapped the sinner label onto them?

When football players thank God for victory, aren't they really saying, "Thank God for making me so great."? Isn't God a crutch, not just for your life, but for your ego?

Without God, would your perception of the world collapse? Or would it broaden beyond your mind's ability to comprehend?

What is God?

What is God?

I think, believers, that God is the opinions that you can't otherwise justify. God is your intellectual *laziness. God is your ego. God is that which you need God to be. God is X. God is the sum of all your willful ignorance. God is a convenience. God is a social adhesive. God is exclusionary. God is your bigotry. God is an excuse. God is your clever ploy to avoid thinking, responsibility and the need to develop a sense of social justice. God is your lie.*

What is God?

God isn't real.

My God is my world. My life. My friends. My family. My time. My lifespan. The breath I draw is God. The photons that hit my eyes are God. The neurons firing in my head are God.

The world is bigger than I perceive it to be, but my world is exactly as big as I perceive it to be, because my perception controls its size. That's how I found a measure of happiness is a world infested by drones, conformity-enforcers, pseudo-spiritualists and other assorted phonies.

Do I have hope? Or have I abandoned the notion? So I believe, as my friend Galen believes, that hope is the last act of a desperate man? Do I echo my hero, George Carlin, when he proclaims that his motto is "FUCK HOPE"?

My attitude towards hope at this point is that if hope helps you, then have hope. If it does you no good, then don't have it. Personally, I don't care about it. I have personal ambitions that I obviously hope are fulfilled, but I have no particular hope for the human race or for our society or any other society, be it in the future or on another planet or wherever.

But that's only my personal choice, because I find that such feelings are useless within me. They will not cultivate properly. Hope doesn't uplift me, because I cannot truly believe it. Trying to hope only makes me more dismal and withdrawn. But if I give up on hope—if I abandon it—then I am happy. And the world is no worse because I abandoned hope.

Dante was wrong. If those in Hell truly abandoned hope, Hell would cease to be Hell! No inferno is hot enough to hurt those who don't care whether or not they are burned.

POLITICS AND OTHER DISGUSTING HUMAN BEHAVIORS

1. THE EMERGENCE OF POLITICS
My friend, scientist and philosopher Howard Bloom, author of *'The Lucifer Principle,' 'The Global Brain'* and *'The Genius Of The Beast,'* is fond of saying that no bacterium is an island.

What does he mean by that? If you put a bacterium alone in a petri dish, it will begin to self-replicate until it has built its own society. It's not an exaggeration to call what the lone bacterium creates a society. It has all of the hallmarks of a society—it has communication, it has resource-distribution, it has division of labor. Do I have a point here? Let's fast-forward and find out.

We, human beings, are great apes. We are most closely related to chimps, bonobos, orangutans and baboons. And what social structure do these creatures adhere to? Do they live in anarchy; a lawless state of total freedom? Are they, as comedian and former libertarian presidential candidate Doug Stanhope claims, unrestricted by any laws but the laws of physics? I'll break the tension immediately by feeding you a spoiler: No.

According to Jane Goodall's website http://www.janegoodall.ca chimps organize into a highly regimented social structure:

Within the community a male hierarchy, ordered more or less in linear fashion, establishes social standing, with one male at the top or "alpha" position. Females have their own hierarchy, albeit much less straightforward. All adult males dominate all females. Most disputes within a community can, therefore, be solved by threats rather than actual attacks.

Bonobo social structure according to science journalist Natalie Angier:

Males form a distinct social hierarchy with high levels of both competition and association.

Given the need to stick together against males of neighboring communities, their bonding is not surprising: failure to form a united front might result in the loss of lives and territory. The danger of being male is reflected in the adult sex ratio of chimpanzee populations, with considerably fewer males than females.

Baboons also live in highly regimented societies with clear dominance hierarchies, as elucidated by studies by Princeton University. Orangutans may be the odd ape out, as they can be fairly solitary, but it's been suggested that females of the species do form loose social groups—they are, however, not a species wherein dominance hierarchies play a very clear part—though certain males do wind up as preferred breeding stock at the expense of the less desirable males. This means that while a regimented social structure isn't in place, competition is still very much a part of life for Orangutans.

Dominance hierarchies are with us from the ground floor of evolution—from the most primitive lifeforms we know of to the closest of our great ape cousins.

Homo Sapiens. We're actually a much more

baffling creature in terms of our social evolution than in terms of our biological evolution. Anatomically modern human beings emerged in Africa 200,000 years ago, but we've only been industrialized for the last 250-300 years. We've only had the internet for about half a century—and it's only been popular among consumers for 20 years or so.

    Let's think about this. We're a 200,000 year old species who just figured out the steam-powered locomotive 210 years ago. We're a species who once hunted wooly mammoth, and now we walk around with gigabytes of information in the pockets of our jeans. How did this happen? Where did this sudden boom of genius come from? How did it spark into being?

    The earliest human beings were hunter-gatherers (like their *Homo Erectus* ancestors before them) who traveled in communities that lived much the same way that the other great apes do—foraging for food: mostly fruit, sometimes meat. The agricultural revolution of about 10,000 years ago changed all that. Human beings no longer had to move from place to place. They could set up permanent residence in some ideal location. They had discovered a brand new subsistence strategy. It was not until this point that we began to seem markedly different than our chimp cousins. Sure, we had always been a little bit better at making tools and communicating with one another, but who could have imagined that we would have it in us to bend the land itself to our will?

So, human beings went from a race of scavengers and hunters to a race of farmers. What social changes accompanied this change in survival strategy? Chiefly this: we went from a society with loose hierarchical distinctions, to a society that all of the sudden had need of tight leadership roles. First, there were village leaders—but soon their were kings and generals, commanding vast swatches of territory and ruthlessly expanding their empires. Soon (relatively speaking), this gave way to the rise of democracy in all of its modern forms. The birth of agriculture soon gave way to the birth of government, which was in turn birth of capital, and the birth of huge income gaps (human X has far more pigs than human Y.) This sort of sounds terrible until you realize that before this inequality existed, everyone was equally miserable.

What happens if you put a bacterium alone in

a petri dish? It builds a society. What happens when you kill the alpha chimp? A new alpha chimp emerges. What happens when you overthrow a government? (HINT: the answer is not, "Anarchy.") A new government emerges. Or several new governments emerge. Hierarchies are inherent to social animals—and a social animal with a society as complex as our own is going to create leaders and followers. We are powerless not to.

You've certainly noticed this behavior even among your own circle of friends. You might not designate someone group leader, but the role is nonetheless obvious to everyone. Odds are you have also noticed that some of your friends are far more submissive and compliant. Anarchy doesn't even work in a group of 6 people, let alone a group of 6 million.

But with the necessary evil of government comes the necessary hilarity that is politics.

2. THE SHADOW OF ISLAM

I come from an older tradition of liberals who wanted to see corruption uprooted from the system and power returned to the people. The new liberalism seems to be about little more than making sure no one gets their feelings hurt.

I don't see it as progressive to lie about the treatment of women in the middle east because you just can't wait to bend over backwards for Islam. The pitiful capitulation of the left wing to Muslim interests is detestable and antithetical to the core value that left-wingers are supposed to stand by: justice. Social justice. Economic justice.

If you stand with those who treat women like second-class citizens, then you are scum. If you are among those who treat women like second-class citizens, then you are not even fit to exist in modern society. You don't meet the minimum requirements for existing on this planet.

I want to make it clear: If you are a Muslim who practices a version of Islam that does not denigrate women, you and I have no problems. But when you look at the policies of Islamic-controlled countries, it's pretty clear that most Muslims do feel that women should have less rights in a great many matters.

3. DEMOCRACY EXPLAINED

In your perfect society, idea X only makes sense if idea Y is also implemented. And idea Y only makes sense if idea Z is also in place.

REPRESENTATIVE DEMOCRACY: You want XYZ! But a lot of people want ABC. The candidates running are LMN and MNO. ABC is voting for LMN, because they think LMN is closer to ABC than MNO. You, as an XYZ, are voting for MNO because you believe that MNO is closer to XYZ than LMN. You're in luck! MNO won the election. So, they're implement societal strategy MNO, but they'll add one of your ideas in to please you—LMNX. But, they have to placate the ABC people too, so they'll implement LMNXA.

LMNXA is, of course, bloated and its ideas are an incongruent mix of the unwanted, the unnecessary and the useless-on-its-own.

DIRECT DEMOCRACY: You want XYZ! But a lot of people want ABC. XACZ is enacted. XACZ is collection of ideas that were never meant to go together. Two conflicting ideas coming to a laughable compromise that creates dissonance for all and pleases no one.

I don't think it makes a difference what sort of democracy we have, because democracy will always lend itself to very strange compromises that murder the efficacy of any plan that any party could ever concoct.

And yet, despite this fault, democracy has performed more admirably than any other system we've yet attempted. Perhaps because we made pleasing the people part of the game that the elites must play to one-up one another. "Look how much more well-fed my peasants are than yours, Mortimer!"

4. SLIP DOWN THAT SLOPE

The problem with debates is that nearly everyone who engages in them will at some point take their opponents ideas to the most extreme possible level. If you're against the death penalty, someone inevitably says, "Well, what if it was your family being brutally murdered with an ice pick?!"

Couldn't I just as easily ask them, "what if your son bludgeoned 3 people to death with a dildo?" You see how not compelling that hypothetical is? Well, yours isn't any better. If you want to slip down a slope, why not let your hand slip down my cock, you mindless bucket of shit?

5. REDISTRIBUTE THAT SHIT!

We have to be like Robin Hood (not the lame

ass Russell Crowe version). We have to rob from the rich and give to the poor.

Here's why: poor people spend money.

We need more spending. We need people to buy buy buy buy buy.

No one can buy when everyone's broke!

However, the rich have never been richer. Now's the time to take their money (which they horde) and give it to lower and middle class people who will spend it. More money in the hands of the middle class means more demands for goods and services, more demands for goods and services means more jobs, more jobs means more people making money.

Be like Robin Hood. Steal from a rich guy, give to some poor, unworthy slob. Then, punch a libertarian in the face and laugh.

If I could create one new law, I'd mandate that no one in a company can make more than 10 times the average salary of the company. For instance, if the average employee makes $32,000 a year, the CEO can make no more than $320,000 a year.

This not only closes income gaps, but it also ties CEO's directly to the success of their companies. Too often now, CEO's are there to collect a paycheck and they don't care if the company fails.

Whatever money they made in or through shares would similarly be capped if it surpassed 10 times what the average employee of the company would be able to make.

The big argument people have made against me on this is that if we passed such a law, CEO's would lose the incentive to run companies because they couldn't get rich. 10 times what a normal employee makes isn't wealth enough for them? 10 times a normal person's income isn't good enough compensation for the job they do? Then fuck 'em, I say.

Ten times average will be good enough for someone who truly loves the job and truly cares about running a company.

6. THE 2012 ELECTION CLUSTERFUCK

I watched a small portion of the 2012 Republican National Convention, and the analysts at the time kept pointing out that the convention was largely an attack on Obama. Many said that this strategy was a bad one, and that the convention should instead focus on building up Romney.

I have to profoundly disagree with these

analysts. Tearing down Obama was do-able. He wasn't the most popular president by any stretch of the imagination. He wasn't despised by all like Bush was, but plenty of people hated him or could be persuaded to hate him.

Making Mitt Romney seem likable, by contrast, would have been a fool's errand. The man was simply not a human being that anyone could ever like. He had the personality of a wet blanket. He lied more often than breathed. He constantly looked confused. He emanated no warmth or humanity. Mitt Romney was best used as a prop—and that's exactly what he was to the Republican party. He was a prop. A variable. An "insert whatever you want to hear here."

So, I think the GOP was wise to make the RNC all about Obama-hating. It's the only card they had—but they still couldn't win with it. Obama probably did more to help Obama than to hinder him. I believe that if the republican party had run a centrist candidate whose policies weren't a total affront to anyone to the left of Ayn Rand, they would have won the election.

The moral crusaders voted for Obama because Obama supported gay marriage and Mitt Romney opposed it—Obama was for the insurance reforms of The Affordable Healthcare Act and Romney was opposed to them (even though he pioneered them as Massachusetts' governor.

But to the left I ask, what good does gay marriage and healthcare do me if I live in a world where my government butchers innocent people and views them as acceptable "collateral damage," jails me for the slightest infraction and doesn't care that my social class is increasingly unable to sustain itself while the richest class control ungodly personal fortunes?

Think about it: every issue where Obama and Romney were identical represents an issue where you had NO CHOICE in 2012.

Obama and Romney were essentially the same. Their differences were all superficial. Pretend. Wedge issues designed to divide the populace and drum up votes.

When it comes to the military industrial complex, wall street, the banks—neither of these men are willing to rock the boat. Obama has not stopped the wars (major combat operations in Iraq actually ceased in compliance with Bush's timetable for withdrawal!), he has not prosecuted one CEO or

Banker in connection with the crash of 2008. He has not made any real effort to close Gitmo. He stopped calling our Patriot Act/domestic spying/drone strike/military occupation bullshit "The War on Terror"—but he has continued to wage it! Obama, at the end of the day, is just a more articulate George W. Bush with a tan.

People who promote voting third party are often derided as idealists—but in my opinion, the people who think any real improvement can come from our two puppet system are the true idealists—that is to say, the ones truly disconnected from reality.

I was going to vote for Obama, but was stopped by the sudden and vivid realization that I was going to help give power to a scumbag just because he pandered to my desire to see gays treated as equals. I decided not to be a part of his re-election. Why should I reward him just because he is crassly manipulative enough to take a handful of decent social positions and policies? His overarching political philosophy bears little resemblance to my own—so why would I make myself an instrument of his power and influence?

Yet it seems that no matter how abominable

the corporate sponsored establishment candidates are, the general public will still back one of them. That's why I shed no tears for this country's plights. Elsewhere in the world, people lay down their lives for Political choice. Here in America, we run screaming from real choice.

I wish that the problem were merely that the American people are being lied to, but the problem isn't that people are being lied to, it's that the people don't give a fuck about what's true. Everyone knows that our justice system is comprised of thugs that brutalize and incarcerate people for non-violent drug infractions. Everyone knows that our government conducts illegal wars all around the world. Everyone knows that moneyed interests have bought the political process and use the government as little more than a means of consolidating money at the top and seeing to it that it stays there. Everyone knows. But nothing happens. That is insanity.

"I gotta vote for the lesser of two evils," they say. Yes—it's the same tired point that has held back social progress for the better part of a century.

Guess what, folks? If you keep voting for evil, the system cannot possibly change. You cannot vote for evil every election and then wonder why evil never leaves power.

I will never again in my life vote for the lesser of two evils! If I choose to vote at all, I will vote for candidates that actually reflect my values. I will not vote for someone who is 95% evil just because he's running against 100% evil.

7. RIOTS

I said in a video shot during the London riots that I really like riots. Many people seemed to get a little upset by that, so maybe a bit of clarification is in order. My love of riots is based on 4 things.

1. *The beautiful aesthetics of a riot.* I enjoy the sight of a massive fire in the middle of a city street—because it's an uncommon sight outside of action movies. Just look at the orange glow it casts on the buildings. Imagine the heat of it, even to someone standing 10 feet away. It's a visually powerful thing—very repellant, but at the same time inviting.
2. *The disruption of the status quo.* I think day-to-day life is a terribly boring thing without some big events thrown in to make life more

fun and fascinating. Now, maybe you guys get your jollies "condemning" riots and pretending you don't enjoy the distraction. That's fine. I won't judge you for that.

3. *I like when the underclass revolts against the rich—even if their revolt is a logically inconsistent, unorganized mess.* Let's face it, these people aren't doing this because they're happy. There is discontent here (in London) and they're expressing it. Are they expressing it logically? No. Because they're uneducated, violent idiots. But damn do they put on a good show.

4. *I like all the arguments that spring up about riots.* Mostly it's a battle between the liberally-minded, who urge that we look at the root cause of these riots and address the social issues that caused them and the conservative minded who don't care why these people are such amoral scum and just want to dispose of them.

One thing you have to say about riots, regardless of how you feel about them, is that a society that can riot is far better off than one that can't.

8. WHY I AM NOT A LIBERTARIAN

Libertarian thought seeks to maximize freedom by limiting or eliminating authority. Now, something you should know about me: I have a diagnosed pathological aversion to authority. I despise cops, teachers, preachers and politicians. I do not like being told what to do. That said—I am a student of human nature and I've seen that human beings need authority. They need it, and will give it readily to whomever is willing to take it. Don't believe me? Then fill up a room with smoke.

If a person is alone in a room and that room begins to fill with smoke, they immediately react. They leave the room. If a group of people are in a room that begins to fill with smoke, they are far slower to react. Why? Because they are looking to one another for leadership. They're looking to see what everyone else does before they act. If one person reacts, all others follow. In other words: if you put human beings in a group, they will seek out a leader.

This is not a terrible burden to the human animal. Our success as a species is owed, pretty much entirely, to our ingeniously complex social structure. Without cooperation there are no bridges, no skyscrapers, no smart phones, no modern marvels. There's just a cluster of humans—or solitary humans, perhaps—living out short lives scavenging for fruit and dreading every winter when the plants begin to die.

    The problem I have with Libertarian thought is this: they believe that market forces can bring us the material miracles of the 21st century. They believe that the freer the market, the more humankind will prosper. The less the government is involved, the more we will all be happy campers. What most of them don't realize is just how unnecessary and recent the "middle class" that most of them belong to is. Corporations don't really need happy, healthy American workers. They can ship jobs overseas. They can hire illegal immigrants. They can pay people less than a human being could live off of. They could create a country with a small upper class and a huge lower class. And there are only two things stopping them: regulations and their consumer base. However, what do they care if they sell one Xbox for $2,000 to a fellow rich person or twenty Xboxes to poor people for $100 a piece? It all amounts to the same. The wealthy can adapt to exist in any society, so long as that society recognizes their wealth. They don't need a middle class—we in the middle class need a middle class.

Another problem with "free markets" is that they place all the power into the hands of the consumer. If we're ever to have high speed railroads, it won't be because of a government mandate—it will be because someone sees the project as potentially profitable. This is all well and good until you consider all the places wherein the profit motive fails to produce peak results: medicine, the environment (no one ever got rich cleaning an oil spill), taking care of the elderly or infirm (no money in that).

Libertarianism, to my mind, is the rich man's way of telling us all: wouldn't life be better if everyone just paid their own way? And the answer is, of course, no. It's much better if we pay some of our way, because the quality of life we lead now is actually largely subsidized by tax dollars. When those tax dollars vanish, life is going to be a lot harder for people who never even realized just how much they relied on the government.

Libertarians often make the moral argument that it's unethical to force people to pay taxes. Force is a big word among Libertarians, and it's not a dishonest one. But let's look at who's being forced.

If we nationalize healthcare: taxpayers—especially those making over $250,000—are being forced to foot the bill. However, now everyone gets to choose between state-run healthcare or private healthcare.

If we nationalize higher education: taxpayers are being forced to pay more—but now kids from low income families can afford higher education.

Do you see how a little force goes a long way to create more opportunities and better choices for everyone?

Let's be clear on one point here: people are dumb and the human race is fucked no matter what it does. We've accomplished some neat things—but the expiration date probably draweth nigh.

Maybe I'm wrong. I hope I am. I'd hate for Shakespeare and Einstein to be snuffed out forever. But here's the thing: we have a choice. We can be ruled by the politicians or the money-holders. Right now, the money-holders pretty much own the politicians anyway and you see how badly things are going.

Let's just stand back for a second and ask ourselves what a corporation wants from us—two things: labor and money. It wants us to work. And it wants us to use the money we made working to buy things.

What does this mean? It means our value is only what we can do and what we can afford. If someone has more money than you in a free market capitalist society, then they have more power. What do politicians want from us? Ignorance and votes. We can conceivably thwart the politician by not being ignorant. It's not likely to happen—but it is possible, and there exists a strategy by which we could conceivably have some power over the politician. However, we the people stand no chance against the businessman. The deeper we let them into the halls of power, the more deeply fucked we are.

The libertarian model of freedom is mostly the absence of authority. But a more accurate measure of freedom is the presence of robust choice in as many areas of our daily lives as possible.

We are, with no doubt, freer than our hunter-gatherer ancestors. Yet--they had no central government! They didn't have the freedom to say, "I'm going to become an artist," or, "I don't feel like gathering today." They either spent every waking minute trying to survive . . . or they died. And that was it for them. Their lives offered them no choices.

Our lives, on the other hand, offer us a glut of choices. What's for breakfast? Whatever the fuck you want! But without a central power structure, without cooperation, without forced taxation—the choices we have as a modern human being would not be possible.

Made in the USA
San Bernardino, CA
20 May 2019